THE 12 LEADERSHIP PRINCIPLES

OF

DEAN SMITH

David Chadwick

D0009460

NEW YORK

For information about permission to reproduce selections
from this book, please write to:
Permissions
Total Sports Publishing
100 Enterprise Dr.
Kingston, New York, 12401

Interior Designer: Elena Erber

Casebound ISBN: 1-892129-08-6
    Library of Congress Catalog Number: 99-63226
Paperback ISBN: 1-930844-25-5

Printed in Canada

To Marilynn

CONTENTS

Acknowledgements

D ean Smith's vision throughout the years has been that the team is more important than the individual. Without the team that helped me finish this project, it would have been impossible. Therefore, as Coach Smith always taught us to thank the teammate making an assist by pointing to him, I point a "thank you" to the following.

My close friend Rick Ray, who read the first draft of the first chapter and put more red marks on it than any teacher I've ever had! Suzanne Waddell, my administrative assistant, for her countless hours of typing, copying, and sending out manuscripts, and for listening to my frustrations. Lee Allison for helping to pull the original manuscript together with Suzanne. Gary Curtis and Ross Bennett, my traveling companions and advisors, for many hours of insight, help, and encouragement.

Connie Reece, my editor, and all the others who read the manuscript and made suggestions — Todd Hahn, Wanna Dayvault, Greg Keith, Ron Smith, Pat McCrory, and especially my Dad (who will always be my hero and greatest influence in life). My Mom contributions are, obviously, equally unmatchable in their way.

My staff, leaders, and friends at what seems to me to be the greatest, most unconditionally loving church in the world, Forest Hill, especially Charles Overstreet. Janet Thoma, Joni Evans, and Grey Coleman, for pats of encouragement along the way!

All the interviewees, whose lives have been touched by Coach Smith, especially Coach Guthridge, whose first year at UNC was my first year.

Coach Smith, who let me write the book despite his desire for privacy and his sincere humility, and for whom it was difficult, knowing people were talking to me about him. I hope this book allows many to learn from Coach Smith, as I have. And that it thanks him for his profound, principle-centered life and leadership. It's a wonderful gift to a leadership-starved world.

Finally, Marilynn, to whom this book is dedicated, my life partner and best friend. She was the first person with whom I shared this idea, and later, when I doubted I could do it, she insisted I go ahead. It was not an easy project, and I simply couldn't have finished it without her. Thanks for the incessant encouragement.

FOREWORD

IT'S HOW YOU PLAY THE GAME

L et's see if you can complete this phrase: "It's not whether you win or lose…"

If you have a modicum of understanding of the American competitive sports scene, you undoubtedly are able to supply the ending: "…it's how you play the game." Reflecting on this thought, the great football coach Vince Lombardi purportedly said, "If that's true, then why keep score?" Lombardi is also credited with having said, "Winning isn't everything, it's the only thing."

Yet are these ideas — that the goal of sporting events is to win or that it is in the manner of playing — mutually exclusive? I don't think so. Perhaps it's because I played for Coach Dean Smith, college basketball's all-time winningest coach. His number-one priority was developing his players as people — teaching us how to play the game rightly on and off the court, showing us how to be persons of integrity. He doggedly believed it *is* how you play the game that counts the most. In fact, if any phrase encapsulates Coach Smith's leadership, it's this one: it's how you play the game.

What then, was the result of Coach Smith's placing the emphasis on how the game should be played?

One number says it all: 879!

That's how many games Coach Dean Smith won over the span of his career. He has won more games than any other coach in the history of college basketball — 879 wins. It's a remarkable feat that makes Dean Smith's name synonymous with winning.

However, in my opinion, it's not just *that* he wins, it's *how* he wins that should be pointed out. It's how he lives his life, how he distributes accolades and deflects praise, how he represents the university, how he cares for his players, staff, and the people with whom his life has intersected through the years that set him apart from others in the coaching profession and leaders in general.

Listen to some of the people whose lives have been touched by Coach Smith:

Donnie Walsh, president of the NBA's Indiana Pacers and a former Carolina player:

> *"I admire this guy more than any other coach because he's not just in it to win games. It's more important that his players come out of there with a well-rounded, well-balanced idea of themselves."*

Larry Brown, coach of the NBA's Philadelphia 76ers and former player and assistant coach under Smith:

> *"Whether you were a starter or a twelfth man, he made us all feel like we were the most important player who ever played for him."*

Rick Pitino, head coach of the Boston Celtics:

> *"It was one of the illustrious careers in all of coaching, and he did it with a great deal of dignity and class."*

Mike Krzyzewski, head coach of Duke University:

> *"He brought out the best in you, because you knew coaching against a Dean Smith team would mean playing at a very high level, a championship level."*

Roy Williams, a former assistant under Smith and now head coach at the University of Kansas:

> *"He has a basketball program, he doesn't have a team. And when you have a program, you're concerned about the kids' entire lives, even after they leave. That's his greatest strength. I've always felt he's the best there is on the court, but he's even better off the court in what he gives to those who come in contact with him."*

Christopher Fordham, former chancellor of the University of North Carolina:

> *"He was more than the best of coaches. He consistently exemplified strong values, respecting his student-athletes, giving academics a very high priority, and encouraging good sportsmanship and civility."*

Michael Jordan, former player and simply the best basketball player in the history of the sport:

> *"The camaraderie he has with his players goes a long way. He's taught a lot of us similar traits and we've moved on as people and as players. That's something we treasure maybe more than our basketball experiences — the things we learned away from the game."*

Bob Knight, head coach of the Indiana Hoosiers:

> *"The very best thing you can say about another person, and you can't say this about many people, is that the more you get to know him the better you like him. That's what I say when someone asks me about Dean Smith. We're good friends. And I have grown to genuinely like him more as I have become more acquainted with him over the years."*

The accolades for Coach Dean Smith could go on and on. Why? What has made this man such an amazingly successful leader? Let's think about what leadership is for a moment.

General George S. Patton defined leadership as the art of getting subordinates to do the impossible. Someone else has said that leadership is the expression of courage that compels people to do the right things.

In the business world, the difference between an effective or ineffective corporation is leadership. In the military, the difference between a good unit and a bad unit is leadership. In sports, the difference between a successful team and an unsuccessful team is leadership.

In his book *Managing for the Future*, Peter Drucker writes that there is no substitute for leadership, and he defines leadership simply as "getting things accomplished by acting through others." Warren Bennis, another who has studied leadership, writes, "Around the globe, we face three threats: the threat of annihilation as a result of nuclear accident or war, the worldwide plague of ecological catastrophe, and a deepening leadership crisis. In my mind, the leadership crisis is the most urgent and dangerous of the threats we face today."

In a world starving for effective leadership, Dean Smith has proven to be a very effective leader. Therefore, I believe there's enormous value in looking at his life and leadership style. As one of his former players, I have seen up close and personal the practical, transferable principles by which he lives. These principles, consistently practiced over almost four decades as a leader, have been the foundation for his outstanding success.

Dean Smith's goal in coaching was not to become college basketball's most winning coach. Indeed, many of us former players had to convince him to surpass former Kentucky coach Adolph Rupp's record. Over and over again Smith had threatened to retire when he was one game behind Rupp. We had to beg him to stay at it, to break the record for all of us who had played for him, if not for himself. Fortunately, he finally agreed.

But breaking the record and winning the most games was not his life's goal. I firmly believe his intent was simply to teach basketball to young men through systematic, disciplined life principles. He would have been happy doing this at any level. The wins followed naturally. Sure, he enjoyed winning. He's extremely competitive. But 879 wins were never the end goal. His players and those who worked for him were his real motivation.

What are these principles Dean Smith imparted to his players? That's the reason for this book. For 30 years I've known and observed him, originally as a player and now as a friend. I believe these principles encapsulate why he is extraordinarily successful as a leader and a man. They are not principles he thought up or invented. They are natural laws, inviolate principles of the human, relational dimension, as real as gravity is to the physical reality. These principles guide civilization. Every positive, meaningful human relationship throughout history observes them. When these laws are obeyed, harmony exists. When disobeyed, there is disharmony, disintegration, and destruction.

Indeed, I would suggest that when people see someone committed to living by these principles, an instinctive inward trust motivates them to follow. Again, I believe this is the real reason for Coach Smith's effectiveness as a leader. Those who know him well consistently see these principles in action. We instinctively sense he is a man of character and ability. We therefore trust him and desire to emulate and follow him.

This is not to imply that he is perfect. He has flaws, some of which I will point out in this book.

In fact, when I approached Coach Smith about his permission to write this book, he quickly granted it.

"David," he said, "it's a free country. You can do whatever you wish."

Then he paused for a moment. Silence engulfed his office. An uneasy look crossed his face. I sensed his discomfort. Finally, he spoke. "Please," he said. Then another moment of silence. "Please don't deify me!"

I won't, although you'll consistently witness my sincere admiration for him. I'm sure, like all of us, he has been forced to live in the fog of deep convictions that at times he doesn't necessarily practice. Surely, like most of us, he has disappointed friends, family, and followers. But when his life has been shrouded in uncertainty, these principles grounded him on a firm foundation and allowed him to persevere. When life has not made sense for him, or when he has made mistakes and been forced to face consequences, these principles continued to guide him.

When I asked Coach Smith about these principles, he said he's not overtly aware of them guiding his life. Yet they're there. They're obvious to anyone who examines his life. Ask any former player. Ask any of his assistants. We would all extend super-human effort for him. Why? We believed in him. We saw his life principles lived out.

Outside of my father, Dean Smith may have had the greatest impact on my life, especially in the area of leadership. That's the real legacy I think he should leave. Leaders in the twenty-first century need to know this man and the principles by which he has lived. Unless someone spends the time to put these insights on paper, future leaders will miss his wonderful example of leadership. That's the reason I have spent countless hours during the last two years writing this book.

As I traveled all over the country and interviewed people and players who have been profoundly impacted by Coach Smith's life, three different core values kept arising that seemed to define his leadership. These three core values are what James Collins and Jerry Porras, in their highly successful *Built to Last*, state are the kind of successful habits every visionary company possesses and drives deep into its corporate culture. First, he placed people above everything else — yes, including wins and losses. People are first in his life. Second, he believes the team is more important than the individual. The individual talents of the player, even if a superstar, must be submitted to the good of the team. Third, personal integrity and character are very important. The leader leads by conviction, care, and character. Then people will trust him and naturally follow.

From these three core values I have identified what I refer to as 12 secrets of successful leadership. If read and practiced, these principles will help anyone become a better and more effective leader.

That's the legacy I hope to leave about Coach Smith to a generation that has admired and venerated him, and to future generations that can learn and grow from his extraordinary life and leadership.

A record of 879 wins in collegiate basketball is impressive. It's a record that may never be broken. Who is the man behind those wins? What allowed him to be so successful? How did he last for so long in today's sports climate of cheating and scandal? How did 97 percent of his players graduate, almost half of whom later attained post-graduate degrees? How have many of these players become fine citizens, leaders in their communities? What are his secrets for successful leadership for the long haul?

It is my privilege to try and answer these questions for you. And in the process I believe we'll discover that it is, after all, how you play the game.

—David Chadwick

1

THE RECIPROCAL
LAW OF LOYALTY

"If you ever need me, call!"

When Dean Smith says, "If you ever need me, call!" he genuinely means it. Every player has heard Coach Smith make this statement at one time or another, and many of them have discovered first-hand that it's true. While he might not think about it in such terms, when college basketball's winningest coach extends the offer to call him, he is expressing the reciprocal law of loyalty to his players.

It's an immutable law. Others have stated it differently through the ages. "You get what you give." Or, "You reap what you sow." Or, "If you want to be loved, be lovable." Or, as the Hebrew scripture says, "The generous soul will be made rich, and he who waters will himself be watered" (Proverbs 11:25). Or, as Jesus said, "How happy are the merciful, for they receive mercy in return" (Matthew 5:7).

It doesn't matter how you say it, the principle still operates the same way: *If you are loyal to people, they'll be loyal to you.* If you put others first, they'll work and play very hard for you. Dean Smith understood and practiced this reciprocal law of loyalty, and every player returned his loyalty. It's not blind loyalty that allows people to take advantage of him. It is a genuine caring for others that fosters mutual care.

When I asked Coach Smith about this principle, he shared with me what led him to reach the conclusion that loyalty to others mattered more than success. "I loved to win and hated to lose," he said. "Yet for years I struggled with something internally. We would play poorly and win, and I'd feel great. We'd play well and lose, and I'd feel terrible. That didn't make sense to me.

"If two of your children were playing tennis against each other, would you really care who won? Is winning all that important in the scheme of things? No. That's why I have ultimately placed compassion above competition. I want to win, but caring for people is much more important to me. I finally concluded that success is not defined by winning or losing, but in doing the best you can, where you are, with what you have."

Putting People First

Why is Coach Smith such a successful leader? I believe it is because he cares first about people. They are his most important products. He knows that everything meaningful in life flows out of relationships, and he steadfastly refuses to manage people as things. Before considering the product, or profit, or goals, or objectives, or action plans — or, especially in his case, wins and losses — he is most concerned about the players who play for him and the people who work with him. He pours his life first and foremost into them. His greatest desire is that they succeed, as players and people, even above his own success.

One of the ways he has demonstrated this desire is by counseling gifted players such as Jerry Stackhouse, Rasheed Wallace, Antawn Jamison, Vince Carter, and, yes, even Michael Jordan, to forfeit remaining years of eligibility for their own financial security. If they had stayed at UNC, Coach Smith's chances for more victories and the golden national championship would have been greatly increased. But he was more concerned about the individual players and their future careers.

After Antawn Jamison and Vince Carter announced their decisions to forego their senior seasons and enter the NBA draft, Ademola Okulaja, another member of that team's starting five, was asked about coaches Smith and Guthridge encouraging both players to leave early. Okulaja said, "It's different here than anywhere else. The coaches really do put us number-one. Many programs squeeze the players out like an orange and then throw them away. But there is respect and honor here — the players have it for the coaches, and the coaches have it for the players. Therefore, there is a certain obligation not to let each other down."

Bobby Jones also knows the value Coach Smith places on caring for people. When Jones was playing for the Denver Nuggets, he began to suffer from epilepsy. The team doctors couldn't figure out what was wrong with him, and the managers just wanted him to play. He was really feeling the pressure. "Then I got a call from Coach Smith," Jones said. "Coach wanted me to come see this doctor in North Carolina that he knew. I did, and he's the one who helped me the most. In fact, he is still my doctor today. When Coach Smith does things like that for people — and he does it a lot — it communicates that he cares for you as a person far beyond an NBA player. That meant a lot to me."

For John Swofford, Coach Smith's practice of putting his players first often meant going to the end of the line himself. Swofford, former UNC athletic director and now commissioner of the Atlantic Coast Conference, was Smith's boss for 17 years. Swofford told me, "Sometimes I think the Carolina basketball program was wrongly caricatured as IBM. It suggested the program was structured like a corporation. A very cold image. It was intended as a compliment because of its wonderful organization. But what got lost was the way Dean always made sure the players came first, before the athletic director, the chancellor, anyone! There were times I would call him about something and he would politely say, 'John, I'm in with a player right now, so we'll need to talk later.' I always understood. He's loyal to his players. They come first. It sent a tremendous message to the players, and it's why they're so loyal to him."

Evidently this reciprocal law of loyalty worked with his assistants too. Bill Guthridge would do anything to protect Coach Smith. For example, when former Maryland coach Lefty Driesell lost to Carolina in a heated game in Carmichael Auditorium, he refused to shake Coach Smith's hand after the game. That was a huge mistake in Coach Guthridge's eyes. He chased Driesell down and chewed him out for his lack of courtesy and respect. Driesell later said, "I really respect Bill. He's a good man, and if he ever got mad at me, well, I must have deserved it."

That's the reciprocal law of loyalty: if you are loyal to people, they will be loyal to you.

Accepting Others Unconditionally

Not only did Coach Smith always put his players first, he also demonstrated that he accepted them unconditionally.

Dave Hanners, who played for Coach Smith in the early 1970s and then became one of his assistants in the late 1980s, says that Smith's loyalty knows no bounds. "Most loyalty tends to float to people who can help you the most. This was not so with Coach Smith. He was loyal to us all, superstar or sub alike."

In 1982 Hanners called Smith and announced he had quit his job because he just didn't want to work where he was any longer. Sensing that Hanners needed to talk about it, Coach Smith had his secretary set up an appointment as soon as possible.

"We talked about what made me quit my job," Hanners said, "and what I planned to do. He was very understanding, but also very tough with me. Frankly, he told me I was fairly stupid to quit my job without having another one lined up. He then evaluated my strengths and weaknesses, not as a player, but as a person. He knew them intimately!

"But when I left his office, I felt great. I didn't have a job. I didn't know where I was headed. But he helped me believe in me. He didn't offer me a job as one of his assistant coaches. That didn't happen until seven years later. I just knew that Coach Smith believed in me, and I would be all right."

What struck me most about my interview with Hanners is what happened while he was talking. It was so powerful it's almost impossible to capture with words. While describing that time in 1982 when he went to Coach Smith for counseling, tears formed in his eyes. He was so overcome with deep emotion that he had to stop a moment and compose himself.

I couldn't help wondering, "Would any of my staff break down and cry when talking about my leadership and loyalty to them? What a supreme compliment!"

That's an important question for every leader to ask. How would those working under you feel when describing their relationship with you? Would they be overcome with deep emotion when describing how you have loved and treated them? Would they unabashedly know your absolute loyalty to them as people first, then as employees? Would they cry when talking about you? If not, why not?

When I asked Hanners why he teared up, he said, "It's this sense of unconditional love from him toward us. The world doesn't understand it. Everything is performance-based. But that's not the case with Coach Smith's loyalty. It's not bologna. I go to the staff meetings. He doesn't say we'll treat the twelfth man one way and the superstar another way. He makes sure every player is treated the same way. It is unconditional loyalty. I think that is what separates him from all the other coaches."

Caring for a Lifetime

Scores of players have found that Coach Smith's unconditional acceptance is not a one-time event. It lasts for a lifetime.

John Kilgo, longtime host of the Dean Smith Show, calls this player–coach loyalty "mesmerizing." The loyalty is so strong, according to Kilgo, that people "want to repay him double. They just don't want to disappoint him. That even goes on long after they leave the university. Along with practically all his former players, I still call him to seek counsel for difficult life decisions. How many people, after they have left a company, would call their former boss and ask for counsel, twenty, thirty years later?"

That's the kind of impact Dean Smith's loyalty has. He influences people for a lifetime.

Richard Vinroot, former mayor of Charlotte, North Carolina, played for Coach Smith in the 1960s. "I feel incredible loyalty to him," Vinroot told me. "But that's because I know how much he cares for me, how loyal he is to me. When I was in Vietnam, he regularly wrote me and checked on my parents. I teasingly say that Michael Jordan and I are the two bookends of the Carolina basketball program. That's how little I played. Yet Coach Smith still treated me like a superstar."

I have experienced this kind of loyalty in my own relationship with Coach Smith. When I talk about his putting people first, about his unconditional acceptance, about his caring for a lifetime, I am describing leadership traits that are personally well-known to me.

I first met Coach Smith in December 1966. He had come to Orlando, Florida, to observe my basketball talent. He was extremely business-like, dressed as if he had just stepped out of *Gentleman's Quarterly*. His dark black hair was slicked back from his forehead. A decided midwestern twang was evident in his voice. I can't remember being that impressed with Coach Smith. He seemed nice enough. A bit stuffy, perhaps even distant. But in the recruiting deluge going on during my senior year, I was not particularly impressed with any coach. I had averaged 22 points and 18 rebounds and been selected first team all-state for the second consecutive year. Some 130 schools wanted my services, and I was absolutely convinced that any school would be lucky to have me.

Was Dean Smith a good coach? At this point, no one really knew. He had recruited some good players in his five years at UNC, but he had yet to win an Atlantic Coast Conference title, much less make it to the Final Four. I was most concerned with his coaching and recruiting ability; I wanted to win, and winning took good recruiting and good coaching. After narrowing my final three choices to Florida, Vanderbilt, and North Carolina, I eventually decided that everything felt right about North Carolina.

So I signed a letter of intent in the spring of 1967. I was so brash about my basketball ability that when I called Coach Smith to announce proudly that I had decided to come to UNC, I also informed him that I wanted to play in the NBA.

Looking back, I realize he must have been laughing on the other end of the line. He had seen me play. He most certainly saw the athletic gifts …as well as the limitations! But he politely said, "Well, David, we want to help all our scholar-athletes to achieve their life's ambitions." That is vintage Dean Smith. He wanted me to be successful, and he did not want to squash my dreams. But he undoubtedly knew my potential. So he gave me a political answer. Every reporter who has ever asked him a pointed question knew what I was feeling. He is a master at refusing to overstate!

In 1967 freshmen were ineligible to play on the varsity team in all Division I athletics. Our freshman team played a 16-game schedule, designed to allow 18-year-olds the opportunity to concentrate on academics without the pressure of big-time collegiate athletics.

I thought I had an outstanding freshman year. We were 12–4, capturing the mythical "Big Four" championship among Duke, Wake Forest, North Carolina State, and UNC. I was the team's leading scorer, averaging 19 points per game, and the second leading rebounder, averaging almost 11 per game. My dream of playing in the NBA kept appearing before my eyes. I couldn't wait for my sophomore year, when I would join a returning team of veterans who the year before had gone to the Final Four. "Why," I thought to myself, "with me and these returning veterans, we could win the national championship!"

Being Honest with Everyone

During the first day of practice of the 1968–69 season, I learned another aspect of Coach Smith's loyalty: he is honest with everyone.

In the first scrimmage, the ball was thrown to me. I wanted to show what I had to offer. I drove to the basket. Jumping as high as I could, I stretched my arm toward the basket, nerves tingling as the ball slipped off my fingertips. I envisioned it nestling softly into the basket to the sound of oohs and aahs from my team members and, especially, from Coach Smith.

You can therefore imagine my stark surprise when the ball ricocheted off my face, spiked downward by Bill Bunting, the team's six-foot, nine-inch all-ACC forward. My face turned red from the ball, but also from embarrassment. I recall a few chuckles. Coach Smith's face hardly changed as he looked at me. "That's not a good shot," he said. "We can do better than that."

The season went downhill from there for me. The team was quite successful. Once again we won the ACC Tournament and the Eastern Regional, and we went to the Final Four for the third straight year. However, I hardly played. I was a seldom-used reserve who was best known around campus as the one who scored the hundredth point in several of our blowout wins.

I was so frustrated that I amassed a list of my concerns; there were about 12. Then I made an appointment to see Coach Smith. I needed to find out how he felt about me. I said to myself, "If he can't convince me that these concerns are invalid, I'm outta here!"

As always, he was very cordial when I arrived at his office. I immediately launched into my diatribe. Months of frustration spewed forth as I ticked off point after point with lightning precision. Each item raised my voice a decibel or two. After about five points, he tried to offer a response. I arrogantly snapped back and said, "Coach, would you mind letting me finish my list. Then we can talk!"

He politely nodded as if to say, "That's okay. I understand."

I finished my list, threatened to transfer, then folded my arms in picturesque exasperation, waiting for some plausible explanation.

To this moment my face flushes in embarrassment when I think about my adolescent outburst. I was an impatient child. Life had not gone as I'd wanted; therefore, I threw a temper tantrum. At the time, however, I felt totally justified.

Coach Smith patiently waited for me to finish. A few moments passed as he looked me over. He had undoubtedly never seen this side of me before. But with a quiet confidence, he said, "David, you are an important part of this program. I think you possess many fine gifts as a basketball player. You have some weaknesses you need to work on. But every player does. If you'll continue to work on those areas, and continue to strengthen the positive parts of your game, I don't see any reason why you can't be a contributor to the success of this program over the next two years. I don't want you to transfer. I hope you'll stay. But if you do transfer, please know I'll always want the best for you."

He waited for me to respond. I didn't know what to say. Then he got up and ushered me to the door. He told me if we needed to talk further, he would be willing. I left confused. My concerns were not fully answered. But he had given me a fair hearing and an honest answer.

For the first time I began to wonder if maybe I wasn't the problem. Perhaps my lack of maturity as a basketball player and as a person was what was holding me back. I wrestled with the possibility of transferring for about a month. Finally, I simply felt this overwhelming conviction that I was supposed to return to Chapel Hill for my final two years. I had made a commitment and needed to honor it.

Between my sophomore and junior years, I worked hard and felt some steady improvement. My junior year was more successful. I moved up to the seventh man on the team. I actually started four games and had some moments when I knew I was a big part of helping the team win a game.

That success my junior year spurred me to work even harder for my senior campaign. In the summer of 1970, I ran and lifted weights every day. I went down to the inner city and played against the best players in Orlando, Florida. I told them they could do anything they wanted to me and I would never complain, never call a foul, even if blood were spilled! I knew I needed to become quicker, stronger, and more aggressive.

I put on 15 pounds. I got tougher. I came back and ran the pre-season mile in five minutes and 26 seconds, the second fastest time on the team and well ahead of any other big man. In the first preseason practice, Coach Smith always allows the seniors to be on the White team, the first team. They stay there until an underclassman beats them out. I stayed there the entire preseason. I played so well they couldn't get me out.

It was a terrific season. We finished 26–6 and won the National Invitational Tournament post-season championship in Madison Square Garden when the NIT was still a very prestigious tournament. We blew by Massachusetts and Julius Erving in the opening round. Then we proceeded to eliminate Providence, Duke, and Georgia Tech for the championship.

I averaged almost nine points per game, was able to start 11 games, and was the first forward substitute off the bench. As I cut down my part of the net after beating Georgia Tech in the NIT championship game, I felt great pride — for playing for UNC and this man named Dean Smith.

What he had told me was true. I worked on my game, became better, and he gave me every chance to show my talents.

But the NBA didn't draft me. I had played very well in the NIT tournament, and a couple of free-agent offers appeared. But my high school dream no longer looked like a reality. It was hard to admit, but I knew I did not possess the physical skills necessary to play in the NBA.

As I began to explore other vocational opportunities, a team from Europe contacted me. They had seen me play in the NIT and were impressed. They flew me over. I tried out. They offered me a contract. I returned home and, naturally, counseled with my dad and Coach Smith. Both thought it would be a tremendous opportunity and adventure. So I seized it. I played in Europe for three years without any regret, three of the most enjoyable years of my life. One was spent in Ostend, Belgium, the other two in Nice, France. I know it's difficult to think about a young man living for two years on the French Riviera, but someone had to do it!

Right before I flew overseas for my first year, I went by the basketball office to say good-bye to all the coaches. As I shook Coach Smith's hand, I'll never forget his final words to me: "If you ever need me, call." At the time I thought these to be perfunctory, hackneyed words from a former coach. I didn't really think he meant them. But I thanked him and went on my way.

That was nearly 30 years ago. At different junctures of my life, I've had to make crucial decisions. Whom do I call? My dad and Coach Smith are the first people. "If you ever need me, call" were not worn-out words from a polite well-wisher, but sincere thoughts from one who has moved from being my coach to my friend. Countless other former lettermen share the same experience. He has said the same thing to them, and backed it up when they called.

In my opinion, it's the primary principle by which he tries to live. Loyalty is foundational to him. When we hurt, he hurts. When we're struggling, he's struggling. Because of this unconditional loyalty, we are very loyal to him. While at Carolina, we play very hard. We adopt his concepts. Then, after we leave, we would do anything to help him and the program. That's why I've called it "reciprocal loyalty."

Empathy for All

Amazingly, those he recruited who went on to sign with rival schools have also experienced this loyalty. For example, Adam Keefe signed with Stanford after being recruited by Carolina. He's a wonderfully gifted athlete, now playing in the NBA. To this day, Coach Smith stays in touch with him.

Mitch Kupchak, former All-American and now the assistant general manager of the Los Angeles Lakers, told me that players from other schools on the 1976 Smith-coached Olympic team also feel like they are a part of the Carolina family and regularly call Coach Smith for counsel. One former ACC player, who spurned Carolina to go to a rival school told me, "The biggest mistake I ever made in life was not to go to Carolina. Yet, recently, I called Coach Smith and asked him to help me obtain a job — and he did! He interceded on my behalf."

Can you imagine a CEO of a major corporation recruiting a young man out of college only to have him commit to a rival corporation, and then continuing to send Christmas cards to him and his parents? Moreover, can you imagine him helping this person years later obtain his dream job? Would the CEO say to these people, "If you ever need me, call"?

Yet Coach Smith does just that. He puts people first. His primary concern is their success, not his. His first priority is to serve, not to be served. He lives by this law: if you are loyal to people, they will be loyal to you.

This principle of reciprocal loyalty helped build IBM in the 1950s. Part of founder Thomas J. Watson's business genius was changing people's perception of salesmen. When the term *salesman* was used in those days, people thought of a shady character trying to do a con job. Watson created an image exactly the opposite of this caricature: a smile, a slap on the back, and a shoeshine. John P. Imlay Jr., a longtime IBM competitor and chairman of Dun and Bradstreet Software said, "He brought real credibility to the sales force."

Watson's values focused on developing closeness among the workers. He hosted family dinners annually for all employees and sponsored intramural team sports, for example. One of his founding principles was "respect for the individual." Many friends who presently work for IBM moan to me about their concern that the bottom line has become the highest corporate value. This may work for the short-term, but I can't help but wonder about being able to sustain long-term morale when reciprocal loyalty is not as important as it once was.

Let me give you a final example of Coach Smith's reciprocal loyalty and his great empathy for others.

When the desire to write this book hit me, I knew I had to have Coach Smith's permission. I therefore made an appointment to see him. Yet as I thought about visiting him, a strange uneasiness overtook me. It grew larger and larger, to the point where I contemplated not going. I searched my soul. What was going on? Finally, I was able to discern what was bothering me. My mind flashed back to 1969 and the time I entered Coach Smith's office with my notorious list of grievances. Did he remember that horrid encounter? Might he possibly hold it against me and not permit me to write this book?

It was a cool, spring day when I arrived at his office. He graciously received me, as always. For the first 15 minutes of our time together, we talked about family. He expressed concern for my aging parents, sharing with me in great pain the agony of watching his mother struggle with Alzheimer's Disease and eventually lose the battle. He had also recently lost his father. He shared how no one is ever prepared for this and exhorted me to enjoy my parents while they were living. Then we talked theology, our similarities and differences. It was a deep, delightful conversation.

Yet I continued to have a gnawing discomfort. I could not believe I was still bothered by my adolescent outburst in his office 30 years earlier! I knew I had to have some peace. I waited for the right opportunity. Finally, a pause in the conversation occurred. I sighed deeply, garnering courage, before I spoke. "Coach, one of my most embarrassing moments was at the end of my sophomore year when I came to you thinking about transferring." I then retold the story in vivid detail, graphically remembering every painful minute.

When I finished, I felt a burden lift off my shoulders. I peered into his eyes. Did he remember? I couldn't tell.

He finally spoke. "David, look behind you."

On the wall behind me hung the composite pictures of all the players who had ever played for him. He continued, "There's hardly one player up there who, at one time or another, hasn't thought about transferring from this program. And most, if not all, have been really mad at me because they didn't think they got enough playing time. We all learn from past experiences. What you did was just part of growing up."

Did Michael Jordan or James Worthy ever complain about playing time? Did George Karl, Mitch Kupchak, Bobby Jones, or Eric Montross ever become angry with Coach Smith? Probably.

In his empathy, Coach Smith tried to put me at ease. I was one of his former players, a part of the Carolina basketball family. Mostly, however, I was his friend. To him, my angry outburst was in the past and did not really matter. He simply reaffirmed his loyalty to me.

Putting the Principles to Work

I have personally learned how to use this principle of reciprocal loyalty in my own leadership. I pastor a large, growing church in the suburbs of Charlotte, North Carolina. The entire budget is around five million dollars, and I oversee a constantly growing staff of more than 40 people and a lay ministry of 2000 people.

In my early leadership, when the church was just entering its growing stage, I did not practice this principle very well and it cost me dearly. For example, a member of the church once approached me with concerns about a particular staff person and his division's effectiveness. I was a bit surprised, for I had heard from others who thought this staffer was doing a credible job. I pondered the problem. Finally, I told the church member to gather more information for me behind the scenes. I thought this would give me all the facts I would need to address the situation.

That was a huge mistake, and it began a disastrous scenario for me.

My staff member somehow heard through the grapevine that I had appointed a behind-the-scenes mole to study the effectiveness of his work. He angrily entered my office and confronted my apparent lack of loyalty to him. He rightly asked why I had not approached him personally about the accusations. In my youthful naiveté, I became extraordinarily defensive. He continued his protest, raising his voice. I got even more defensive and raised my anger level to match. He reciprocated.

I was guilty of first desiring to be understood instead of understanding. It's one of the cardinal sins of a leader.

Our relationship, from that point forward, slowly but surely deteriorated and eventually fractured. Mistrust grew. His job performance began to dissolve, and it became inevitable that he would have to leave. Moreover, he shared his frustration with friends on the staff. His disgruntlement began to spread throughout the entire group. Others thought, "Well, if David would do it to him, why wouldn't he do it to me?" There was a malignancy of mistrust everywhere!

What is most depressing to me about this story is that most of the rumors proved to be unfounded and wrong. Now not only did I have a fractured friendship (which, fortunately, later was healed), not only did an important part of our work become paralyzed for several months, not only did mistrust proliferate among other staff, but a potentially valuable and gifted person was irrevocably lost to this organization.

It was a terribly painful time for everyone involved. In the months that followed, I seriously evaluated what had happened. I chewed on the problem over and over. I read management books by the dozen. Yet none of them gave me the kind of answer I wanted.

From where did the solution ultimately come? It came when I simply asked, "What would Coach Smith have done in this situation?" When I asked myself this question, I remembered his leadership principle of reciprocal loyalty. Why did we play so hard for him? Why did we mostly experience unity on his teams? It was because we felt his unyielding loyalty to us, and we reciprocated with extraordinary effort.

In light of this principle, I began to ask myself, "How should I have handled this? What did I do wrong? Second, what can I initiate for now and future staff members, based on this leadership principle, to help insure this never happens again in my own leadership?"

Looking back, I realized I should never have asked the critic to find out whether the rumors were true or not. I should have immediately called the staff member into my office, affirmed my loyalty to him, told him what I had heard, and lovingly asked for his response. If anyone should have gathered information for me, he should have been the person. Then I could have easily managed him, the process, the information, and his division's output. The relationship would have remained solid. His job could have been saved. His potential would not have been threatened. And the rest of the staff would not have experienced a creeping paralysis that took months to overcome.

At that point I had to perform damage control. But I also wanted to formulate some preventive medicine. So I gathered the rest of the staff together, honestly shared my mistake, asked for their forgiveness, and then tackled with them how we could prevent this disaster from ever happening again.

We decided as a staff to live by the core value of reciprocal loyalty. We covenanted together to live by a principle outlined by Jesus in Matthew 18:15 on handling conflict. It simply says that if you have something against someone else, go to that person, face to face, immediately, before the sore has a chance to fester, and try to reconcile the problem. If that doesn't work, go again with two others who sense the same problem. If that doesn't work, then it's time to get the entire board involved. But that's the absolute last resort.

Moreover, we communicated this commitment to the members of the congregation (who would be similar to the customers in another organization). We said we were committed to exemplifying for them how to handle conflict. We also said that if anyone ever came to one of us and complained about another staff person, we would tell the complainer he had 24 hours to go to that person or we would tell him what was said. We wanted all our members to learn and practice reciprocal loyalty. We believed it to be very important as a principle, and we still do to this day.

It has been 11 years since my disloyal faux pas. But I did learn from my mistake. Every new staff person who has come on board since then must agree to this covenant of loyalty. Together, as a staff, we carefully go over this principle during the interview process with each prospective staff member. We ask if they totally understand it, if they have any questions about it. If they balk in any way, we know they won't fit on our staff.

Not once since we initiated this covenant principle has anyone ever rejected the idea of reciprocal loyalty. In fact, they have been extraordinarily thankful for this process to be in place. I think good staff people instinctively know the importance of such loyalty and yearn to live by it.

Over the ensuing years, relational bumps have naturally occurred. A few have even been strangely similar to the one experienced 11 years ago. However, not once has it caused any relational or organizational damage. In fact, when a staff person once said something that seemed to suggest disloyalty, two other staff people went to him and confronted him before the problem ever got to me. He immediately recognized his potential disloyalty and went to the other staff person and asked for forgiveness. The issue was never discussed again.

Since initiating this principle, staff morale has been extremely high. Our commitment to teamwork and one another has never been better. The congregation takes this principle very seriously. Gossip has abated. Unity is incredibly high between staff and church members. Moreover, during the last 11 years our membership has doubled and the budget tripled. We're now in the middle of a huge expansion program that will build an auditorium to seat 2,000 people.

What's the result? Charlotte and the whole area have benefited from our ministry, largely because we have learned and are practicing the leadership secret of reciprocal loyalty.

My youth pastor and close friend, Robbi Fischer, shared a story about this principle of reciprocal loyalty. Several years ago the church was going through a transition time, refocusing our vision. We decided to reach out to those who would normally not attend any church.

Fischer began to attract a large number of "fringe kids," as we call them. Some had green hair. Others had tattoos. They were not your normal church kids. Fischer received a lot of criticism from parents who worried about the effect these fringe kids might have on their own.

"During a parent's committee meeting," Fischer said, "David walked in the room. He knew it was tense and emotional, and he knew that if he said something it might open himself up to more criticism, which he was also receiving for this transition. But he walked up to me, put his arm around me, and said before the group, 'You've got to know that I am one hundred percent behind the youth ministry and the desire to show God's unconditional love to today's teenagers.'

"That meant more to me than a thousand words of affirmation behind the scenes. It not only began to calm the storm in my ministry, but it gave me a clear picture of what David had been talking about in our covenant of reciprocal loyalty."

It's amazing that when the congregation senses this commitment to loyalty among the leadership in the church, they tend to relax and quit their complaining. It's the same way when a child senses that Mom and Dad are on the same page; they feel secure and quit complaining. But if they sense tension between their parents, they start acting out.

From where did I learn this easy and practical leadership principle? From Coach Smith. Peter Drucker, the contemporary management guru, once said, "Efficiency is doing the thing right, but effectiveness is doing the right thing." Dean Smith is very effective as a leader. Why? Because he does the right thing. He cares for his players above all else. People are his most important assets, his most valuable product, even ahead of wins and losses.

Profits or People?

What would happen in companies and organizations across America and the world if leaders would see their people as their primary product? What would happen if every leader desired above all to see his underlings succeed and be happy in life? What would happen if reciprocal loyalty became a core value of all managers and their organizations?

Here is a good example of the potential of this principle to affect a corporation. Slumping sales of athletic shoes and the sullied reputation of sports figures have forced Nike and its competitors to examine whether they want to continue signing athletes to multi-million dollar promotional deals. Expense cuts, even layoffs, loom on the horizon. What should be done?

At Nike's quarterly international sports marketing meeting in January 1998, managers discussed the relative merits of signing the two most promising players in the NFL draft: Ryan Leaf versus Peyton Manning. Someone finally suggested the company save money and not sign either one. Sources at the meeting told the *Oregonian* newspaper that Nike CEO Phil Knight said he would rather cut athletes than lay off a single employee.

I personally think Phil Knight is thinking rightly. If he did this, would Nike's profits shrink or diminish? I dare imagine that a company's profit margin and success would exponentially increase when others are placed first. Right principles, especially being loyal to people and caring for them above all else, will only foster closeness and a greater desire to succeed.

All other life and leadership secrets outlined in this book are rooted in this one principle of reciprocal loyalty. If this one falls, like dominoes, all the other ones do too. If the leader is not loyal to his underlings, teammates, and associates, success, especially over a long period of time, simply will not follow.

I certainly understand that sometimes, albeit painfully, leaders are forced to prune people for a variety of different reasons, from deregulation to new technologies to international trade, to mention a few. No one can argue that leaders have a duty to their shareholders. But is profit the entire ethos of business? Is "shareholder value" our only concern? Aren't there other expressions of value, especially our people?

Or, as Collins and Porras suggest in *Built to Last*, successful visionary companies never fall prey to the "tyranny of the OR." They believe you can pursue caring for people and profits, both, at the same time, all the time. As Don Peterson, former CEO at Ford, said in 1994, "Putting profits after people and products was magical at Ford." Yet Ford was still very profitable!

Is profit the leader's primary duty? Isn't there also an especially high calling to the workers? Aren't they our most valuable asset? In a different time, the chairman of Standard Oil said in a 1951 address: "The job of management is to maintain an equitable and working balance among the claims of the various directly interested groups: stockholders, employees, customers, and the public at large."

More and more leaders today are becoming concerned that profit is now much more important than people. They are concerned that the mean salary of the contemporary chief executive is approximately 190 times the salary of the normal worker, up from 40 times in the 1970s. Nearly 50 percent of America's stock is owned by one percent of Americans. In fact, according to the Federal Reserve, 60 percent of American families own no stock at all.

Perhaps leaders today would be wise to study such leaders as Robert N. Johnson, the founder of Johnson and Johnson in 1886. His vision for his company was "to alleviate pain and disease." By 1908, this view evolved into a business strategy that put the satisfaction of employees ahead of profits for shareholders. J. Williard Marriott Jr. said the motivating factor in his company "is not the money" but the pride of accomplishing a task and doing it well. He points out that profit to shareholders naturally follows.

Coach Smith had an interesting way to "downsize." If he thought someone wouldn't ever play and sensed that to be very important to him, he'd not only encourage him to transfer but ardently help him find another school. He'd always be listed thereafter as a Carolina letterman, be a part of the family, and receive annual notes from Coach Smith. One such transfer encouraged a high school hot shot in his area to attend UNC, not the school to which he had transferred. That's the way to downsize! The law of loyalty still works!

Winston Churchill once said, "The inherent vice of capitalism is the unequal sharing of blessings. The inherent virtue of socialism is the equal sharing of miseries." There's no magic solution for how to prioritize people and profit and still keep shareholders happy. But I think one way is to examine Coach Smith's reciprocal law of loyalty.

Dean Smith coached for almost 40 years with unparalleled success. The results are now legendary, for the ages. They will be talked about and analyzed for decades to come. Why was he so successful? Because he placed others before personal gain. He lived first by the law of reciprocal loyalty.

By the way, when I left his office that spring day when he granted me permission to write this book, I shook his hand and exchanged final pleasantries. You know what his final comment to me was?

"As you develop this project, if you ever need me, call."

I knew he meant it.

Thought for the Day

If you are loyal to people, they will be loyal to you.

Game Plan

- Put people first
- Accept others unconditionally
- Care for them over a lifetime
- Be honest with everyone
- Have empathy for all
- Care for people who produce the profit

Team Practice

- What does loyalty mean to you?
- How do you demonstrate loyalty in your personal life?
- How do you demonstrate loyalty at work?
- What can your organization do to foster loyalty among customers, shareholders, and employees?

LOYALTY PROSPERS IN A FAMILY ENVIRONMENT

"I'll never be your real father, but I guess we do have a large Carolina family."

It was no different than any other practice session, at least that's what we thought. The 1971 season had been a surprise. No college basketball pundit ever dreamed that at this point in the season North Carolina would be on top of the Atlantic Coast Conference standings. Yet we were, a testament to Coach Smith's leadership ability and our playing together as a team.

We were all seated in our chairs that day, ready for Coach Smith to enter. We regularly assembled like this, either to go over the practice plan, study an upcoming opponent, or watch game film. The coaches entered the room and everyone fell quiet. But Coach Smith did not begin talking. Something was eerily wrong. He remained quiet for several seconds. Tears filled his eyes. We had never seen him like this. He cleared his throat, in obvious discomfort. The silence was suffocating.

"Gentlemen," he finally began. "This is very difficult to talk about. But we're all family here." Every man inched to the edge of his chair.

Personally, I expected Coach to share that he was accepting a job somewhere else. Or perhaps someone on the team had gotten into trouble and needed to be disciplined. I would never have imagined he was about to share that *he* was the one in trouble.

"I know that if I'm struggling, it is going to affect you," he said. "I wish it wasn't so, but I know it is. Since we are family, I want to share with you what's going on in my personal life." He then shared with the entire team how he and his wife were having problems in their marriage. He said it had been going on for some time and that it was tearing both him and his wife apart.

Then, in the final phrase, he admitted he didn't know what eventually would happen. They were seeking counseling, but he freely confessed that the marriage might very well end in divorce. Then he bravely asked if anyone had any questions. He said he wanted to be above board in every possible way, and if anyone had any reasonable questions, he would try to answer them as honestly and forthrightly as possible.

I don't remember if anyone had any questions. Frankly, I don't remember much more about that afternoon than what I've described. I remember feeling sadness for him, his wife, and the children. They did ultimately divorce, and he shared that, too, when it finally happened. It was a significant failure for him, one I'm sure he wishes he could change.

But what I do remember very vividly about that day is the fact that he openly shared his own private struggles because he believed we were a family. He believed that his personal life affected us, so we needed to be abreast of what was happening in his life.

As I have examined Coach Smith's leadership skills, I have come to realize that one of the reasons for his great success is that he created a family environment for his players. In fact, he created a family before he created the team. That's the context in which loyalty prospers: family.

Functional families care about one another and openly share both their failures and their successes, their happiness and their hurts.

The first thing Coach Smith did to create that family environment was to be vulnerable before his players and staff.

John Maxwell, in his book *Developing the Leader Within You*, recognized this same principle. He wrote:

> Long ago I realized that in working with people I have two choices. I can close my arms or I can open them. Both choices have strengths and weaknesses. If I close my arms, I won't get hurt, but I will not get much help either. If I open my arms I likely will get hurt, but I will also receive help. What has been my decision? I've opened my arms and allowed others to enjoy the journey with me. My greatest gift to others is not a job, but myself. That is true of any leader.

This is what Coach Smith was doing when he shared with the 1971 team about his own marital problems. He gave us the gift of himself.

Through the years, the family atmosphere Coach Smith created has evolved to the point where he has become a surrogate father to many of his former players.

Being a Surrogate Parent

Take Michael Jordan, for example. After his junior year Jordan left UNC to enter the NBA. "I was unsure, nervous, scared — going into a situation I didn't know if I was ready for," he told me. "But Coach calmed me down with a fatherly attitude, taking me under his wing and teaching me a lot of things about being an adult."

Then came perhaps the most trying moment of Jordan's life. His father was mercilessly and senselessly gunned down while sleeping in his car. Since that happened, Jordan has turned to Coach Smith over and over again for counsel and condolences. How does Jordan characterize his relationship with Coach Smith? "Since my father's death we have grown even closer," he said. "He's very much like my father to me. I love him."

Jordan may be the most famous player to regard Dean Smith as a surrogate father, but he is far from the only one.

Buzz Peterson, the 1981 North Carolina high school player of the year and present head basketball coach at Appalachian State University, also views Coach Smith as a father figure. "Every major decision I have made in my life — sports, marriage, everything — I have gone to him. When I was about to be married, he listened to me and gave advice. You almost feel like you are one of his kids.

"When I won my first conference game here at Appalachian State and I walked into my office early the next morning, the phone was ringing. It was Coach Smith congratulating me on my first conference win. That meant a lot to me. It was as exciting for me as the win itself."

Perhaps the most poignant story I heard came from Pat Sullivan, a former player and a graduate assistant under Coach Smith. Sullivan's alcoholic father left the family when Pat was about 15. "During my sophomore year," he told me, "I was really struggling with it. My mom was great. She handled it well. But I just didn't feel comfortable talking to my mom about something like that. I didn't know where to turn. I was also angry. Did he not love us? I just didn't understand."

Then Coach Smith came to Sullivan and initiated a conversation about his father. They started to meet regularly, to help Sullivan work through his feelings.

"He told me my dad had a disease," Sullivan said. "It wasn't that he did not love us. It wasn't that he chose alcohol over the family. Coach Smith gave me a bunch of tapes to listen to. Some of them were spiritual and some of them on the medical side. Then, every week or two, he would call me into his office and simply ask how I was doing. He asked me if I needed to talk to some of his friends who were psychiatrists. Without him, I would have stored a lot of grief and anger in my heart."

Gradually, Coach Smith convinced Sullivan to contact his father. "He made me think about how hard it probably was for my dad not to talk to me, how hard it must be to try to overcome a problem with no one supporting you. That really got me thinking. I realized I needed to love him even though he was sick. So I wrote him a letter and we corresponded after that. I was really glad Coach Smith encouraged me to do that."

Sullivan's father passed away during his son's senior year. They had never had the chance to talk personally again, but they had stayed in touch through mail. "I came home late from the movies one night and received the news from my roommate," Sullivan said. "The next morning, Coach Smith wanted to see me. He said at least my dad wasn't suffering any more, and I would be able to experience some closure on the situation.

"Later, I realized that in all those times we talked before my dad died, Coach Smith had been preparing me for it. By helping me deal with my anger and encouraging me to contact my dad, he was preparing me for whatever might happen, even his death. Coach refused to let me feel guilty. He simply helped me understand that my dad was sick. That was the greatest thing he helped me understand."

When I asked Sullivan if Coach Smith was like a father to him, he immediately responded, "Oh, yes. I look at him like my father. He knew about my dad's problem during the recruiting process. I think he knew even then that he would need to care for me during my years at Carolina. He is just so caring."

Similar sentiments flow from one of my lifelong friends, Bill Chamberlain. Few people would have expected us to become close. Chamberlain was a gifted, highly skilled, six-foot, six-inch African-American forward from the inner city of New York; I was a six-foot-seven white preacher's kid from the suburbs of Orlando, Florida. But, for whatever reason, we became fast friends at Carolina. He spent several hours with me sharing about his relationship with Coach Smith for this book.

Chamberlain was the most valuable player in the 1971 NIT tournament. He scored 34 points in the final game, exhibiting a dazzling display of skill and athleticism. He went on to play in the old ABA and the NBA. When he talked about his relationship with Coach Smith, there was a hushed awe in his voice, an almost reverent tone. At times he even became misty-eyed. "I remember," he said, "how much my parents liked him. He came across as a person with great character and integrity, unlike many of the other recruiters. His approach was humble, warm, and genuine. He came to my parent's apartment in Harlem, which I'm sure was not an easy trip for him!"

Chamberlain shared some of the different episodes in his life when

Coach Smith's friendship meant a great deal to him. "Probably the most difficult time in my life was when my wife of seventeen years, Wheatley, died in November 1988. We were very close and really loved each other. She had just given birth to our second child. About five weeks later, a congenital brain aneurysm erupted and she died. That night Coach Smith was on the phone to the hospital. He was there for me.

"It's like a blur right now as I talk about it because of the pain. But Coach was constantly there," Chamberlain said. Coach Smith called the hospital, came by the house, and attended the funeral. "He basically held my hand. I was an emotional wreck. We had no previous knowledge she was sick. We were amazed that she didn't die in childbirth, exerting so much pressure. But she didn't. And when she did, Coach Smith was there, by my side, caring for me, loving me like a father loves his son.

"During all my life's trials and circumstances, Coach Smith was like a father to me. I don't know too many players who go to a university and feel like their coach is a father they can call whenever they need him. But I feel this way about Coach Smith. He will be like my father until one of us leaves this Earth. There's nothing I won't do for him, and I sincerely believe he feels the same way about me."

We have already seen how the family environment created by Coach Smith fosters the kind of reciprocal loyalty Chamberlain talked about. But one thing we have not examined is where this whole concept of family originated.

Treating Each Other Like Family

That's an important question, because this feeling of family extends to anyone who has ever played for Coach Smith. For example, I had a difficult time trying to obtain an interview with James Worthy. He was a very successful NBA player and is now a nightly sports commentator for college basketball's television broadcasts. He is a very visible figure, with the NBA and many staff people protecting him from a clamoring public. All my attempts to have him comment on this project failed.

Finally, Mitch Kupchak called Worthy and told him that I was a former player and what I was trying to accomplish with this project.

Worthy readily agreed to see me. When we finally did the interview, he apologized for my difficulty in reaching him. He said, "If I had known you were in the family, I would have agreed to meet with you immediately."

When I interviewed Coach Smith, I probed him regarding his efforts to create this kind of family environment. He admitted he had intended to develop that atmosphere. "It probably goes back to the way I was raised," he told me. "We are all products of our environment in one way or another. I was raised in a relatively strict home. I spent four hours on Sunday in church, even though I oftentimes didn't want to go. But I learned most all my values from a very loving mother and father."

Bill Guthridge, Smith's longtime assistant and eventual successor, agreed with this assessment. When I asked Coach Guthridge about the Carolina family feel and why it existed, he immediately surmised that Coach Smith brought his personal family commitments into the UNC family philosophy. The closeness of his own family influenced his approach to coaching and his emphasis on treating each other like family.

John Lotz, another of Coach Smith's assistant coaches, also believes that Coach Smith's understanding of family was the foundation for leadership principles like loyalty and placing others above self. Lotz said, "I have no doubt it came from his own family. His mother and father were really Christians in the true sense of the word. We are talking about a different era — the thirties, when Coach Smith was being raised. They were strong Baptists and believed absolutely in doing the right thing. His parents were both schoolteachers and undoubtedly hammered these principles into him from an early age. They taught him to do the right thing and then to teach others how to do the right thing."

I believe Coach Smith learned most, if not all, of these principles about the value of family through his own family. These principles gave permanence and power to him, and he passed them on to us. They were delivered to him within the context of a family. He delivered them to us within the same context.

Bill Chamberlain shared another story with me about the family environment Dean Smith created at Carolina. As family members are apt to do, Chamberlain created some real headaches for Coach Smith.

One occurred during his sophomore year, when Chamberlain became involved with the Black Student Movement and the cafeteria workers' strike.

"The university had asked them to work thirty-nine and one-half hours per week," Chamberlain recalled," so they wouldn't have to be paid medical benefits. Other white workers weren't treated that way, and I simply thought that was unfair. I threatened not to play, even to transfer, if their needs were not addressed. Coach never tried to dissuade me from my commitment, even though I know he must have been wondering what to do.

"One day I went by his office unannounced to talk about the strike. He was in a meeting with the chancellor of the university. When his secretary buzzed to tell him I was outside, Coach asked the chancellor to leave so he could talk with me. Interestingly, he totally supported my position. He even ended up signing a petition demanding rights for the cafeteria workers, which they eventually got.

"When I left his office, the chancellor was still sitting outside. Then he went back in Coach Smith's office to continue their conversation. Can you imagine? A player causing him as many headaches as I did being more important than the chancellor! But we were more important to him than anyone except his own personal family. Yet, come to think about it, we were his family!"

As I listened to this story, a question kept sweeping over me: would any of my present employees ever say this about me? I thought especially about those who are younger on my staff, some of whom come from broken homes and dysfunctional families. Do they look to me as a potential father figure? Do I give them reason to do so? What could I do to make my work environment more like a family instead of a mere organization?

Evidently I'm not the only leader to be asking such questions. One man who is trying to create a family environment in a corporate context is Don Carty, CEO of American Airlines. According to Knight Ridder reporter Dan Reed, Carty is trying to change a long history of autocratic management and to make American a company that its people can love because it is a company that cares about and responds to their needs. To that end, he has spent much of his first seven months as CEO preaching to workers and managers alike about the importance of building not only professional skills and competencies, but also the enthusiasm and the love and respect for each other that he believes has been missing within America.

As more and more Generation Xers, many of them from negative family structures, enter the corporate workforce, managers and leaders need to be consciously creating a positive family environment. It's impossible to calculate how much more productivity takes place on a team or an organization when people feel like they are family, that they belong to one another.

But how do you go about creating a family environment? So far we've covered some of the general principles: being vulnerable, becoming a surrogate parent, treating each other like family. Let's look now at some of the practical things Coach Smith did to help create and develop this family feel.

Developing the Family Feel

Dave Hanners offered some interesting perspectives on Coach Smith's family approach to coaching basketball. Not only was Dean Smith like a surrogate father for the players, Hanners suggested, but he also set up, either intentionally or intuitively, a system where other members of the immediate and extended family played roles in the program. For example, assistant coach Bill Guthridge became the players' favorite uncle. He was much more relaxed than Coach Smith, with a gentle and engaging sense of humor. One of my favorite stories about Coach Guthridge's sense of humor involves Michael Jordan. At the zenith of his popularity in the early 1990s, Jordan was in Chapel Hill in the basketball office. Coach Guthridge ran into him in the hall and wryly said, "Michael, I haven't seen you in a while. What have you been doing since you left Chapel Hill?" Because of Guthridge's gregarious, humorous personality, some of the players felt more comfortable going to him with different problems. This may be one reason why the transition was so successful when Coach Smith retired. The players lost dad, but their favorite uncle stepped in to replace him.

Then there is Phil Ford, one of Coach Smith's greatest players and an assistant for many years, another uncle who brings something else to the family. He's a bit younger, therefore he can joke around with the players more easily. Hanners said, "Phil is great at loosening the players up. He runs out on the court with them at practice, telling them that he is number-one. He points to his jersey, retired over one of the baskets, and tells them that when he played they had a play called '12 lob.' They would just throw the ball toward his jersey and he would go up and get it and slam-dunk the ball. The kids get a kick out of that." Hanners suggested to me that when Coach Smith chose his assistants, he looked for personality traits he didn't have, in order to give balance and better meet the needs of the players.

"I think he even chose secretaries with the family idea in mind," Hanners continued. "To me, they are like four surrogate mothers or aunts. They possess the maternal instinct. When the guys come in the office, they tell the secretaries things they will never share with the coaches, things like problems with their girlfriends. Sometimes they don't want us to think that they have everyday problems. I believe Coach Smith knew the family needed moms, so he hired secretaries who are not only wonderful administrative assistants but who could also supply the maternal side of the family environment."

Hanners had a final insight into how Coach Smith helped develop the family feel. "I even wonder if in the design of the office space in the Smith Center he didn't think through developing this family thing. The kitchen is in the center, as are the players' mailboxes. In order to get a drink or get their mail, they have to walk by the secretaries' desks. I've always wondered if that were intentional, forcing the players to deal with their need to interact with a mother figure. Many of these guys come from fatherless homes and mom is the strongest person in their lives. Perhaps this design just had the right feel for him in developing this family commitment among us all."

Think about these practical things Dean Smith has done to create a family environment. Do you see these same ideas in your sphere of influence? How many leaders would recruit a staff knowing certain ones might fulfill different roles in the family? How many would begin to design office space in new buildings in order to maximize a family feel? What a revolutionary thought!

Long before the Smith Center came into existence, however, Coach Smith was nurturing a family environment. During my interview with him, he gave me another insight into how he tried to create family. He reminded me how, every Thanksgiving, he would invite any player who wanted to come over to his house for Thanksgiving dinner.

"Oh, yes," I said. "I did that a couple of times."

He then told me he personally would have never gone over to Coach Allen's house for an event like that when he was playing under him at the University of Kansas. "I would have preferred to be with my friends."

"I was just trying to get more playing time!" I replied.

We laughed. He said the Thanksgiving tradition was an attempt to create a family atmosphere among the players, "although I never wanted it to become a buddy-buddy affair. That was the tension for me. I wanted a family atmosphere, but I knew we couldn't be too friendly at this point. That would happen later, after you graduated."

Caring for Your Personal Family

During this conversation about family, something absolutely amazing happened. The phone rang. Coach Smith looked puzzled for a moment. He said, "I don't understand. I gave explicit instructions not to be interrupted." The phone stopped ringing. We continued the conversation. Then it started ringing again. He was not puzzled any longer.

"Excuse me for a moment," he said. "That must be my private line. It's either one of my children or another former player. They're the only ones who have my private number. You're the only ones who can get to me any time you want!"

He picked up the phone and said, "Hello." Then he smiled. "Hi, Kristen." He covered the phone and said, "It's my daughter. I'll be right back with you." Then he spent the next several minutes counseling his teenage daughter about something that was important to her.

I laughed to myself. I had been furiously studying different articles written about Dean Smith trying to find a way of illustrating my conviction that his former players are like family to him. I had looked everywhere but couldn't find one. Then he gave me the illustration during the interview. Coach Smith said the only people who possessed his private telephone number were his own blood children and players like me!

From his perspective, we're all in the same general category: we're a part of his extended family. That's the way he looks at us. That's why, if we ever need him, we can simply call. That's why we all love him so much.

Do most bosses feel this way about their employees? Or do they feel people are objects to help them reach the bottom line? What would happen in workplaces if employers fervently tried to create an atmosphere of extended family? What would happen if employers created an environment of honesty where all employees, the boss included, could at times open their hearts, share their struggles, and know they would be embraced, not rejected? Employers, do your employees look to you as a surrogate parent? Are your employees learning to treat each other like family, and learning to care for their own personal family, by following your example?

Through my years as the leader of a rapidly growing and changing church, I have learned that if my staff's families are not functioning properly, the staff will not perform well in their jobs. Therefore, I have tried to take this leadership secret from Coach Smith and initiate a family commitment among the staff at the church I pastor.

How do I do this? I try to create times away from our work and all of its tensions, times where the staff simply get to enjoy each other. Occasionally, four times a year, volunteers answer the phones while everyone goes to the local coffee shop for fun and fellowship. The leader over the different divisions must always buy. We'll also have picnics at the park during the week together, go bowling, or go to a movie together. One leader regularly takes his staff to Laser Quest, an arcade where people shoot laser guns at one another. I imagine this is a great opportunity to work out frustrations!

Another thing we do weekly is to divide into groups of six or so for the purpose of sharing any hurts or pains in our lives. Then we pray for one another. It's amazing how this 30-minute weekly meeting together significantly increases our family feel. You also have managers and support staff and maintenance people together sharing one another's burdens. Barriers break down quickly when you're helping someone else carry his huge problem.

However, probably the wisest thing I've done in fostering a family environment is to force, yes, mandate, that my staff take a day off every week to be with their families. I hold them accountable for this, and I become angrier at a careless oversight in this area than an inadequate monthly report. It's because I understand just how important this personal time is for establishing a stable, successful family.

For 19 years, I have had a standing appointment with my wife. It has reaped tremendous rewards. She knows that once a week, every Friday over breakfast, we will have two to three hours together to talk about whatever we need to talk about. On many occasions, it has been marital salvation. My staff could share similar testimonies. In all my years of ministry, we've not had one staff divorce.

For my staff, this mandatory day off every week communicates to them the importance of building their own families. If they have healthy families at home, then they not only help develop the family commitment at work, but they will perform better without personal distractions draining their focus.

Some are saying today that business is at war with family life. Not so at Half Price Books. It is presently the largest used-book dealer in the United States. What has been its key to success? By moving into cities where its employees and their family members desire to move. Again, developing this emphasis on personal family life will be especially meaningful to leaders who must manage GenXers. With their broken homes littering their past, they will be especially desirous of the ability to nurture their own families. Moreover, with women moving into corporate leadership positions, work and family life have become mandated with such features as working at home, flexible hours, and daycare at the work place.

Charles Handy is one of Britain's leadership gurus. In his latest book, *The Hungry Spirit, Beyond Capitalism: A Quest for Purpose in the Modern World,* Handy studied how contemporary organizations can adapt to modern situations. In a chapter called "The Citizen Company," he concluded that businesses must operate like communities. He described people who work for these companies as "citizens" in today's workplace. I think he may need to go a step further. We're not only communities with citizens, but families with individual family members — and the workplaces are either functional or dysfunctional!

Continuing the Family Relationship

The wall of the kitchen near Coach Smith's office is covered with photographs of former players, their wives, and their children throughout the years. A picture of my own three children is there, with Coach Smith holding my youngest, Michael, when he was just a few months old.

One particular picture is insightful. Michael Jordan's son, Marcus, is seen as an infant wearing pajamas. A phrase written on the pajamas nicely encapsulates the principle covered in this chapter: "All I do is eat, sleep and root for the Tar Heels." Marcus, too, is a part of the family!

And the most important part of this family relationship is that it continues long beyond a player's days at Carolina.

One of the most telling of all the stories from former players regarding their feelings about being a part of the UNC family came from Rick Webb, a seldom-used substitute who played for Coach Smith in the late 1960s. Here is the story Webb shared with me for this book.

"On October 5, 1996, I was involved in a life-threatening car accident. I was in intensive care for twenty-three days, undergoing seven difficult operations. Although I truly believe I was saved only by God's grace, my experiences under Coach Smith's leadership and being a part of the Carolina basketball family helped me recover.

"Although I played very little, tough practices and arduous conditioning reinforced important life lessons: humility, tolerance, patience, compassion, understanding, consideration, kindness, and, most important, love. I also learned the power and peace associated with prayer. Coach Smith was a great believer in prayer before and after games.

"The Carolina basketball family was there to support me throughout my recovery. Coach Smith wrote and checked on me regularly. Other players really cared for me with their prayers and presence in my time of need."

Everybody reading this book — everybody on the planet, it seems — knows who Michael Jordan is. Few would recognize the name of Rick Webb, however. He was never a superstar, just a seldom-used college basketball player who would have been long forgotten in the ordinary scheme of things. But the Carolina basketball family is not ordinary. And

30 years later, Rick Webb is still a part of the extended family, still as loved and respected and cared for as Michael Jordan. That's because Coach Smith made us a family.

"Most athletes learn how to endure and play through physical pain and suffering," Webb told me. "But coping with the mental and psychological aspects of debilitating injuries requires you to draw from experiences learned through life's many trials and tribulations. My experiences with Coach Smith, his influence, and the Carolina basketball family, helped me gain the strength, determination, and patience necessary for my continuing recovery and changed lifestyle."

Is there a leader in the world who would not love to have that statement made about them by someone who has been under their tutelage? Wouldn't it be thrilling to see how your leadership has positively affected someone during life's trials? This influence evolves most naturally in a family environment of caring for one another. It's an environment that the leader creates.

Every leader who desires to be effective should ask, "Are my people my most important product? Are they like a family to me? Do they care for one another like a healthy family does? Are the people under my leadership learning principles that can be used when tragedy hits? Would they describe our workplace as being like a family?"

Charles Dickens once said, "No one is useless in the world who lightens the burden of another." I'm convinced that most often takes place within the context of a family commitment. I believe Coach Smith understood this too.

After all, leaders come and go. But families will always be necessary.

Perhaps Phil Ford summed it up best when he said, "I always tell Coach that he's the only father in the world with three hundred children, and only five of them are his own."

Thought for the Day

Loyalty prospers in the context of family.

Game Plan

Create a family environment by:

- Being vulnerable

- Being a surrogate parent

- Treating each other like family

- Caring for your personal family

- Continuing the family relationship

Team Practice

- What do you do to create a sense of family in your team?

- How do you demonstrate vulnerability?

- In what ways do you treat each other like family?

- How do you demonstrate concern for others' personal family?

FRIENDS ARE FOREVER

"But when you leave, you're my friend."

When I asked Coach Smith to describe his leadership style, he never paused. "I was a benevolent dictator. I was the leader. There was no doubt about that. I came up with the practice plans. I controlled everything. But I hope I did it all with some benevolence. I tried to control with compassion."

I had to smile. He did run everything with an iron grip. There was no dialogue in practice. He did not seek our input regarding issues. It was either his way or the highway! Coach Smith would never hesitate to throw someone out of practice, or make them run extra sprints if he thought their actions were hurting the team.

No, there was no doubt about it. He was unquestionably in control. Yet he *was* a benevolent dictator. We knew he deeply cared for us, individually and collectively.

Coach Smith reminded me that each year he let us become just a little bit closer to him. "Wasn't it your senior year, David, that we started letting the seniors make some of the rules and regulations outside of practice?" I nodded.

"Well, I knew that most freshmen come on campus as high school hot shots, and I had to begin to knock some of that out of you. That's why on road trips, freshmen had to carry the projector and do other grunt work. That's why sometimes I would be extremely hard on you as a player. In a real way, I had to tear you down to build you back up. Then, as seniors, you became leaders yourself. You had earned the right to be closer to me."

What he said rang true with me. That was exactly what happened in my years under his leadership.

"But," he continued, "after you left, after you graduated, you became my close friends. Everyone talks about my loyalty to my former players. But I don't treat you any different than I would a close friend. Since you're my friend for a lifetime, of course I'm going to be there when you need me. Of course I'm going to care for you. And I hope that you would do the same for me, simply because we're friends."

In the last chapter I showed how many former players consider Coach Smith a surrogate father. When I asked if he thought of himself in this way, his answer was immediate. "No, I couldn't replace your parents. They did the job of raising you. You are who you are primarily because of them, not me. I look at you and all the former players as my friends. I am your ally, your friend."

I would respectfully disagree with Coach Smith on this point: he is like a father who grew to become our close friend.

But perhaps he is stating something that is even more important than the family feel he created among us. Perhaps he is stating that, beyond family, we possess something that is greater to him: friendship. Above everything else he wants us to be his life-long friends.

My conversation with Coach Smith made me reflect on my relationship with my own father. I grew up in a loving family. However, make no mistake about it, my dad was the boss. He was a benevolent boss, but he was still the boss. In my early childhood years, I remember him as this huge figure. He was in control and I was supposed to obey him. I knew he loved me. I knew he cared for me. But there was still some distance, caused mostly by my awe and respect for him.

Then, as I moved into adolescence, I experienced him more and more as my father. We started doing more things together. He would come to my games. We would share thoughts about different subjects. We grew closer, and as the years passed I moved from experiencing him as a benevolent dictator to knowing him as a loving father.

Now, as an adult, I know him as one of my closest friends. The depth of our relationship far transcends his being the one responsible for raising me, or giving me guidance, as a father is supposed to do for his child. Now, he is simply my close friend.

Similarly, that is what former Carolina players have known with Coach Smith. He is a father figure who became a close friend.

And the basis of this friendship starts with the fact that he accepts us for who we are and respects us as individuals.

Accept People for Who They Are

His acceptance of and respect for people as individuals is apparent in episodes such as the recruitment of Danny Manning. When Manning was a senior in Greensboro, North Carolina, everyone thought he was a lock to attend North Carolina. However, Larry Brown, then head coach at Kansas University, hired Ed Manning, Danny's father, as one of his assistants. The younger Manning committed to Kansas soon thereafter and later led the Jayhawks to the national championship.

Many Carolina people have never forgiven Larry Brown for the Danny Manning situation. They thought it cost UNC many victories and possible national championships. It's one of the first things they bring up when referring to Larry Brown. But Coach Smith never mentions it. Whenever he talks about Larry, it's always with great respect. Why? Because they are friends and that's the way friends treat one another.

This kind of friendship has a higher priority for Dean Smith than celebrating victories. When North Carolina beat Georgetown in 1982 for the national championship, most fans missed something that happened on the court as the Tar Heel team erupted in celebration. Coach Smith immediately looked for John Thompson, Georgetown's head coach and his close personal friend and assistant on the 1976 Olympic gold medal team. Coach Smith ran to Thompson and hugged him. Reading his lips, you could see him ask, "Are you okay?" His first reaction was empathy for his friend, not joy for the national championship. Only after Thompson acknowledged that he was okay did Smith return to celebrate with his players and assistants. No wonder John Thompson remains a close friend to this day!

One player who has experienced this kind of acceptance and forgiveness from Coach Smith is Phil Ford, undoubtedly one of Smith's greatest individual and team players. Ford graduated from high school in Rocky Mount, North Carolina, with amazing credentials. His basketball acumen was outstanding. Practically every school in the country tried to recruit him, and many different coaches all promised him a starting position and plenty of playing time. That's quite alluring for any high school star. It's a difficult carrot not to bite when thinking about signing with a school.

Then Coach Smith came to visit him. Ford had always been a North Carolina fan. But he also knew he was a fabulously gifted point guard who could impeccably run Coach Smith's famous Four Corners offense. So he waited for the pointed pitch, specifically how he would almost certainly start and be given tons of playing time in his first season.

To Ford's astonishment, Coach Smith promised nothing. Instead, he told Ford he might have to play on the junior varsity his first year in order to grow as a player and totally understand the system. The only promise Coach Smith made was that he would be treated fairly.

"That kind of set me back," Ford later recalled. Indeed, he didn't like it one bit. However, slowly but surely, he began to see this honesty as something positive, especially with help of his mother. She said, "Phil Jr., if he's not out here promising you that you will start, that means that if you go there and work hard and do the best you can, then he won't be out promising your job to another high school player." Acknowledging his mother's wisdom, Ford said, "If you think about it, that made a lot of sense."

Ford did sign with Coach Smith and North Carolina. His career was spectacular. Not only did he lead Smith's teams to dozens of victories and to ACC championships, but to the championship game of 1977. He became an All-American and a John Wooden Award winner as a senior. His future sparkled. He was a first-round draft choice in the NBA and became rookie of the year in 1978.

Forgive Human Frailties

The future seemed limitless for Phil Ford, until his third season as a professional. A broken orbital bone of his left eye caused double vision. He could never regain the magic in basketball that had led to so many successes. Slowly, depression crept over his soul. He turned to alcohol. He consumed more and more. It didn't take long to realize that full-blown alcoholism had ensued. His career began to erode. He was being pushed out of the league and onto the streets. It was the darkest moment in Ford's otherwise brilliant life.

Yet it was also at this moment that Ford discovered Coach Smith was not just a benevolent dictator or his surrogate father, but his friend. When word reached Coach Smith about Ford's dark despair, he immediately picked up the phone and tried to track him down. He wanted to meet immediately and find out what needed to be done for Ford to become well.

Ford described it this way. "Coach Smith saved my life. It was like he was saying to me, 'Hey, I'm here for you. It's going to be me and you. You and I will solve this problem together.'" Hope began to flood his soul. He saw that life still had purpose and that, with Coach Smith's help, he could overcome this demon tormenting him.

Coach Smith began making phone calls to rehabilitation centers around the country until he found what he thought was the best one. Ford entered the clinic and began the long, difficult road toward recovery. That was more than 10 years ago. A couple of years after the recovery process began, with his life back on track, Ford became an assistant coach at UNC, where he stayed until Coach Smith's retirement in October 1997.

Why would Coach Smith do this? Yes, Ford was a former player, an awfully good one. Yes, he was part of the Carolina family. That's important. But I would suggest that the primary reason Coach Smith believed in and helped Ford is that he is his friend. That's the way friends act. They forgive our human frailties and reach out to help us when we need it.

When James Worthy, North Carolina's All-American forward in the early 1980s and later an all-pro with the Los Angeles Lakers, talked about Coach Smith as his friend, he said, "You notice it right away. There's nothing you can't talk to him about. The door is always open to his office. If you needed a day off to study for a final exam, he would give you the day off to study.

"But the friendship really happens after you graduate, when you are living life on your own. You really grasp how much he cares after you leave. I am much closer to him right now than I have ever been, and the closeness grows every month. When I was playing, he still sent me good luck mailgrams on opening night. He remembers anniversaries when *we* can't remember them. And it's not public relations. It's sincere. It's Coach Smith. He is our friend and he regularly communicates it."

After James Worthy made headlines with a much-publicized bad decision, another former player expressed his exasperation with Worthy to Coach Smith. Smith quickly defended Worthy, saying that no one could really understand all the pressures and temptations of being an NBA superstar. He, too, lamented Worthy's poor choice, but he was very unwilling to throw stones. Coach Smith encouraged empathy toward Worthy, not judgmentalism.

Desire the Success of Each Individual

Another way Dean Smith expresses his friendship is by wanting the best for his players as individuals, desiring their success, no matter what it costs the team. Yes, the team was all-important. But we heard him say regularly, "The individuals on the successful team are the individuals who receive the most attention."

Justin Kurault, a team manager in the late 1980s, shared insights with me about Coach Smith's friendship for his players and managers during his tenure. Ostensibly, Kurault was not essential for the program to remain in the top 10. Yet, at the end of his senior year, Coach Smith took aside Pete Chilcutt, Rick Fox, and King Rice, his senior starters, and Kurault, the team manager. He asked the four of them how he could help them fulfill their life desires.

Kurault told Coach Smith he wanted to coach. Coach Smith responded, "Well, if you don't want to make any money, I'll see what I can do for you."

"So I spent the summer working Coach Smith's camp and a couple of other camps. Finally, I found out that Coach Smith helped me get the assistant's job at Davidson. It's hard to believe he would do all that for someone like me — just a manager. But he told me, 'You're my friend. That's what friends do for one another.'"

Richard Vinroot, a letterman in Coach Smith's early years and former mayor of Charlotte, North Carolina, told me this story about how Coach Smith placed his respect for individual players even above victories against Atlantic Coast Conference foes. When King Rice was the starting point guard, he went through a very difficult week. He had a campus altercation that resulted in his arrest, and he had a short stay in jail.

That week, Carolina was playing Maryland in Chapel Hill. At that time there was no proof that King Rice was culpable, so Coach Smith allowed him to start.

He played terribly. Carolina lost. Tar Heel fans are usually loyal to a fault, but they mercilessly booed King Rice when Coach Smith left him in the game.

Afterward, Vinroot was in Coach Smith's office. He was frustrated with the loss and launched into a diatribe against Rice. Coach Smith's irritation slowly but surely rose. He finally said, "Richard, you don't know all that King has been through this week. You don't know his frustrations and what is going on in his mind. Yes, I started King tonight and played him practically the entire game. But, frankly, King's self-esteem at this point is far more important to me than whether we win a basketball game."

Isn't that amazing? Coach Smith was more concerned with one player's self-worth than winning a basketball game. By the way, King Rice went on to win many games for Coach Smith and Carolina. Today he's also successful in his chosen career. Could it be at least partly because of the confidence he gained from Coach Smith in this Maryland game? One game was sacrificed to help win many others and to help a kid grow in his life.

Justin Kurault added this insight about the King Rice incident. He said that after the campus altercation, Rice was so embarrassed about it, he didn't respond to two different attempts by Coach Smith to reach him. When they finally met together, Coach Smith firmly reminded Rice that he cared about him as a person first. Coach Smith also told him that he was his friend, and he would stick by him no matter what.

One of my most intriguing interviews in working on this project was with Bob Knight, head coach of the Indiana Hoosiers. North Carolina squared off against Indiana in the 1981 national championship game in Philadelphia, Pennsylvania. Knight has repeatedly received flak in the press for his antics and treatment of players.

Coach Smith had mentioned to me that he and Bob Knight were friends so, on a lark, I wrote Knight and asked if he would like to comment about Coach Smith's leadership for this project. He responded immediately and said he would really like to express his thoughts about Dean Smith.

The interview took place on a snowy day in early March 1998, in Bloomington, Indiana. It was on a Monday of the first week of the NCAA tournament — not the best time for his total concentration. However, when he finally did sit down with me, Knight could not have been more cordial. He began by trying to teach me about theology and particularly the differences between John Calvin and John Wesley. Fortunately, we quickly moved to the real reason for the interview. (I think I could have beaten him in a theological debate, but I honestly did not want to try!)

When Knight began to talk about Coach Smith, his voice changed, becoming almost reverent. He said, "Over the years our friendship has deeply grown. When somebody asks how I get along with Dean Smith, I tell them we are good friends. And I also tell them that he is one of the few, if not the only, person I know, that the more I became acquainted with him, the more I wanted to know him."

Knight continued by telling me a story he had never told before. "We were eating in Chapel Hill," he said, "after an NCAA officiating meeting in Greensboro we both had to attend. The restaurant was very crowded and there was a light atmosphere. When the check came, Dean grabbed it. I said, 'No, I'm taking us to dinner.' And he said, 'No, I'm taking us to dinner.'"

Knight swore and said, "Dean, I am going to pay for this." He put his hand on Coach Smith's wrist and demanded the check.

"I told Dean I'd seen this kind of stuff from him before and that he could pay tomorrow night. We could argue about it again the next night too, but I was paying for dinner tonight. And I took the check from him.

"He didn't know that I heard him, but while I was giving the credit card to the waiter, he leaned over to my wife, Karen, and said, 'You know, he is the only person in the world that I would let do this.' That's the way Dean is. He's unbelievably generous.

"What I was saying by paying for that dinner was that I really appreciated being with him. And by letting me pay, he was saying he really enjoyed being with me too. I thought that was really a nice thing for him to say about our relationship."

Coach Smith and Knight have known each other now for 33 years. They are close friends. At no time was this in greater evidence than the summer of 1998, when *Sports Illustrated* published a rather scathing article about Coach Knight's antics and treatment of players. The next week, in the letters to the editor, who wrote a letter to defend his friend? Dean Smith. He said:

> Coach Knight was and is a brilliant technical coach and teacher of skills.
>
> Knight will not cheat in recruiting, although many coaches in the Hall of Fame with him have been on NCAA probation.
>
> Knight demands that his athletes get their degrees.
>
> Every school would like to have a coach who wins games, whose players have been recruited legally and who graduate, and who brings in millions of dollars to support the many men's and women's programs that cannot support themselves.
>
> I am not aware of any player who has graduated from Indiana who is not grateful to Coach Knight for his experience with the Indiana basketball program.

When Richard Vinroot criticized Bob Knight over his news-making antics with players, Coach Smith angrily came to Knight's defense. He pointed out many of the things Knight has done and continues to do for his players.

For example, after Landon Turner, a star in Indiana's 1981 national championship season, was crippled in an automobile accident, Knight came up with money to help defray his medical expenses. He continued to counsel Turner through a time of deep, dark depression, when Turner learned he would be in a wheelchair for the rest of his life. Smith wanted Vinroot to know the kind of positive things Knight had done that did not receive publicity.

Wouldn't any of us do the same thing for a true friend? Wouldn't we publicly defend a friend if we thought he was wrongly accused? If a close friend of ours had fallen into alcoholism, wouldn't we do anything within our power to help him return to a normal life? Wouldn't we want to help a close friend find a job and fulfill his career ambitions?

We would do that for our friends, but what about our employees? Why do we not allow them to get close to us?

Allow People to Get Close

Yet think about what would happen if employers, over the years, allowed employees to become friends.

Certainly there will always be the tension of how to be a boss and a friend at the same time. Someone naturally has to be the captain of the ship. But should this prevent a meaningful friendship from taking place, a friendship that could enhance, not hurt, the bottom line?

I believe there is a way to do both!

In my own ministry, I oversee dozens of people. The 15 who work most closely with me are called "the program staff." Daily we interact and struggle with difficult issues. They are very gifted, competent people who have been working with me for as few as six and as many as 12 years.

Yet, through time, they have not only been close work associates, but have become my closest friends. If I am hurting, I could go to any one of them and seek help; they would gladly give it to me.

Yes, I am the leader. They understand that. If tough decisions need to be made, I must make them. Yes, I do their annual performance evaluations. Indeed, yearly I call a select few of them into my office and they do a performance evaluation on *my* leadership! This has proved to be extremely helpful to my personal and professional growth. I know they are concerned about my leadership. They want the church to succeed. And I receive their input because I know it is coming from people I value as my friends.

Conversely, I sometimes have to say difficult things to them, pointing out areas that need improvement in their ministry. But that's understood. They understand that's the way the system has to work. But they are also my friends, and this close friendship allows us to work more competently together. We believe in each other. We care enough to confront when necessary. But we also love each other because we are friends.

We also hang out together. We love to spend time together as families. Annually, we spend three days at the beach together. My son's closest friend is the son of one of my staff persons. We simply like each other. And it has carried over to the workplace.

I believe that employers and employees can be friends. It is the foundation of the best possible working relationship. But for this to happen, you must see people as your highest aim, your most important product.

It's my conviction that out of these meaningful friendships your best product is produced. Ronald R. Fogleman, the Joint-Chief-of-Staff for the United States Air Force, once said,

> You ought to treat your machines as if they were people, but never treat your people like machines. You need to care for your resources, but you have to treat people like people. To become successful leaders, we must first learn that, no matter how good the technology, people-to-people relations get things done. People determine our success or failure.

When win number 879 occurred in Winston-Salem in the NCAA tournament in March 1997, allowing Coach Smith to move ahead of

Adolph Rupp as college basketball's all-time winning coach, every former player who could be there was present. I had already committed to being with my family in the mountains, or I would have been there too. As I watched the game on television and saw the record become his, my eyes were moist. I was profoundly happy for him and excited to know I had been a part of his program. Mostly, however, I was proud that I could call him my friend.

Right before the game ended, the former players who were there slipped out of the stands and lined both sides of the tunnel leading to the locker room. As Coach Smith left the coliseum, his eyes also became moist as he noticed each former player. He stopped and shook their hands. He knew they had all helped allow this moment to occur. Overcome with emotion, he thanked all of them for what they had meant to the university and to him. He thanked them for being there and, mostly, for being his friend.

Perhaps Phil Ford best summarized it for all of us who played for Coach Smith when he said, "I had a coach for four years, but I got a friend for life."

Thought for the Day

A friend is always there, no matter what the situation.

Game Plan

- Accept people for who they are
- Forgive human frailties
- Desire the success of each individual
- Allow people to get close

Team Practice

- What actions do you take to build lasting friendships?
- To what extent can a leader be friends with his/her followers?
- How important are friendships in the workplace?
- What could your organization/team do to build stronger relationships?

THE TEAM BEFORE THE INDIVIDUAL

"The individual must submit his talents for the sake of the team."

A t the beginning of his career, many critics doubted Dean Smith's coaching ability. His early teams did not succeed. After a particularly painful ACC loss in the early 1960s, some of the student body even hung him in effigy. He ostensibly turned it around from 1967 to 1969 with three straight Final Four appearances. But many still felt Smith achieved this because of his ability to recruit talent, not because of his coaching ability.

Then came the 1971 season, my senior year. The pundits predicted doom and gloom for Carolina basketball. Charlie Scott, our All-American, had graduated following a disappointing 18–9 season. His replacement was an aggressive, fearless point guard named George Karl (now coach of the NBA's Milwaukee Bucks). On the surface, it seemed like a replacement that would make the team worse, not better. We were slotted to finish next to the last, right above Clemson.

Before the season began, Coach Smith preached that teams, not individuals, win games. He constantly exhorted us to play as a team, to believe in his vision of the team. He said that if we did, we would surprise everyone. He was so convinced that no individual was greater than the whole, that every player bought the idea. None of the critics imagined we would succeed like we did. Yet we were ranked in the top 15 teams that season, winning 26 games, the Atlantic Coast Conference regular-season title, and the prestigious NIT championship in New York.

Art Chansky, in his book *The Dean's List*, which chronicles all of Coach Smith's seasons, said the 1971 season did two things for Carolina basketball. First, it showed the philosophy of team above the individual worked. With no apparent superstar, the team was imminently successful. Second, it convinced every Carolina recruit thereafter that if they played by the Smith philosophy, they would win games. They caught the vision.

Bobby Jones told me, "Coach Smith somehow, someway, made us believe that if we followed his philosophy we would win. By the time I was a senior, if he'd told me to go to the corner and stay on my hands and knees until the play was over — if he said we would win by doing that, I would have done it. We knew putting the team above the individual worked. We knew that was his vision. And we did whatever he told us because we believed in him."

In my opinion, this concept of team may be Coach Smith's greatest gift to basketball and society. It doesn't matter whether you're coaching a sports team, managing a corporation, being a parent, or leading a Boy Scout troop, creating a cohesive team is critical.

In his book titled *Business as a Calling*, the respected lay theologian Michael Novak quotes David Packard of Hewlett-Packard: "When a group of people gets together and exists as an institution that we call a company, they're able to accomplish something collectively they could not accomplish separately. Together they make a contribution to society."

When a leader melds a group of people into a team, and when the leader inspires that team with a vision, then great things begin to happen in an organization. The team will be far more productive working as a unit than as individuals. B.C. Forbes, founder of *Forbes* magazine, once said you spell success: T-E-A-M-W-O-R-K.

Critics have tried to demean Coach Smith's dogged vision of the team as being more important than the individual. A regularly recurring joke has been that Dean Smith is the only person ever to hold Michael Jordan to fewer than 20 points a game.

When I asked Kansas coach Roy Williams about this, he became mad. "The people who make those kind of comments don't know what they're talking about. Michael was double- and triple-teamed at every opportunity. Then the shot clock was initiated during his college years. In 1982, when we won the national championship, we averaged scoring in the sixties. Everyone was trying to control tempo by controlling the basketball. Plus, we saw zone after zone, and Michael had not yet developed his great jump shot. But go ask Michael about his greatness and the foundation he learned under Coach Smith. He is a great player today because he learned to play team basketball at North Carolina."

As much as Coach Smith's former players genuinely love him, that affection was only partly responsible for his success. We played hard for him because we believed in his vision. We believed it won basketball games. We believed his philosophy worked. And his record of 879 wins proved it beyond a doubt.

What was Coach Smith's vision? It's very easy to encapsulate: "No individual person is greater than the team." He would frequently say to us, "If you want personal recognition, you should play tennis, golf, or run track." He was totally convinced that the team playing together is the goal of basketball. He even told me, "I wish that some year some coach who had gone twelve and fifteen would be named coach of the year, just because he did a wonderful job coaching the team. It's society that stresses wins and losses. But that's not what's most important: it's the individual submitting himself to the team."

Even before the team is assembled, the leader must realize that it is his vision that gives direction. Then he must surround himself with gifted, competent people to achieve this vision.

Justice Oliver Wendell Holmes once boarded a train in Washington, then realized he had lost his ticket. The conductor recognized him and said, "Don't worry, sir. I'm sure when you find it, you'll send it in."

Justice Holmes replied, "Young man, the question is not 'Where is my ticket?' but rather, 'Where am I supposed to be going?'"

Coach Smith clearly knew where he was going: the team would be more important than the individual. The team would win games. This was his vision, and he stated it almost daily.

Management gurus say that a leader needs to restate the vision every 28 days to keep the team focused on it. I have learned in my own organization that our vision similarly needs to be repeated at least that frequently, or people tend to forget it. We therefore talk as often as possible about the vision of being a contemporary church trying to express old truths in new ways. We use bulletins, inserts, up-front announcements — whatever possible — to communicate the vision.

Coach Smith did the same. I can hardly remember a practice session without the vision of the team above the individual being stated in some way. Often the thought of the day, printed at the top of the daily practice plan, had to do with this vision. The assistant coaches regularly stated it. While studying game film, we would hear the team vision quoted over and over again.

Every year it was this vision that united each new team. This vision was reflected in a sign that hung over the door leading to the court in Carmichael Auditorium. It simply read, "United we stand, divided we fall."

Teams win games. Individuals playing selfishly lose them.

Burt Nanus, president of Visionary Leadership Associates and professor emeritus at USC Graduate School of Business Administration once said, "Every leader needs a vision. And the process never ends. The role of direction-setting never ceases. The leader is constantly reassessing the vision, refining it, and allowing it to evolve and grow."

That's what happened in 1971. We totally believed in Coach Smith's vision of a team. We truly believed that if every individual subordinated his gifts for the sake of the whole, we could accomplish anything we desired. The vision created synergy and the victories piled up. Every team under Coach Smith's tutelage has similarly caught his vision.

I had the privilege of being in Chapel Hill when Vince Carter announced his decision to forego his senior season and turn professional. It was not the best decision for the North Carolina team. However, it was the best decision for Vince Carter, and that was why Coach Smith encouraged him to do it. During the press conference, Vince shared why he was going to the NBA. He went on and on about how it would help him fulfill personal and professional goals.

Finally, Coach Smith interrupted Vince in mid-sentence. "He'll also help the team," Smith said. Everyone associated with the Carolina program chuckled. Even during Vince's momentous occasion, Coach Smith could not resist reminding his superstar that the team was what is most important.

Let's look now at some of the different ways Coach Smith allowed this team concept to develop. Most, if not all, of these ideas are transferable to different leadership situations. They have been for me in the church.

Teach What's Important in the Vision

I asked Coach Smith how he initiated this concept of team first into practices so we could best understand it. How did he teach the vision? "You should know that one," he responded. "It begins on the defensive end. If a team plays good defense, it can always be in a game."

We spent the first three weeks of preseason practice mostly learning team defense. He taught us "help" defense, how we all needed to help one another. Then he taught pressure defense.

Coach Smith used a particular trick to prove the need for pressure defense to initiate the action. He would hold a dollar bill between his thumb and forefinger. He then bet us that we couldn't catch the bill when he dropped it. Of course, we all tried to do it. And each time we failed. It was a demonstration of his cardinal basketball theory: "Action beats reaction."

That's probably why Coach Smith considers himself primarily a defensive coach, why he advocated strong, man-to-man, pressure defense. He said, "The offense will always have the advantage against a defense that just sits there waiting to be attacked, waiting for somebody to take a shot. So, if you're on defense, you've got to go get the ball. Let's not take what they are going to give us; let's take what we want."

After I played for three years in the European professional leagues, John Lotz, who had become the head coach at the University of Florida, invited me to become a graduate assistant in his program. I gladly agreed. I was with him for two years and received a graduate degree in counseling while there.

During my first year at Florida, Coach Smith spoke at the Gator team banquet. At the beginning of his talk, he noticed that I was sitting in the audience. He said, "Oh, I see that one of my former players is here and working on the staff, Dave Chadwick. I want to tell you that Dave was one of the finest offensive players ever to play at North Carolina. He could really score."

My chest widened. I was so proud to hear Coach Smith say these things about me. I looked around to see who was glancing at me.

Then he continued, "But, unfortunately for Dave, I'm a defensive coach."

My balloon popped. I melted in my seat. Everyone laughed — at my expense!

But Coach Smith was right. I could score, but defense was difficult for me. And he was a defensive coach who believed the concept of team began with defense. He taught this from the first day of practice forward.

That's not to say that offense wasn't important. He also taught that no matter how good the defense was, the other team would score. But he knew that if we played good defense, we could stay in the game.

Coach Smith's offensive schemes are as carefully studied and copied as his defense. Let's face it, he's a brilliant coach, offensively and defensively. However, in teaching the team concept, he began with defense because it was the most important part of the vision. He could never know, from night to night, if the offense would score. Players who are gifted offensively never know from one night to another if they are going to have the touch or be in the zone. Coach Smith knew, though, that a team could play hard defensively every night. This could be a constant. He therefore developed the team concept first by focusing on defense.

Jack Welch, CEO of General Electric, believes in this idea of focusing on what's most important with your team. Since Welch took over in 1981, GE has moved from a cumbersome bureaucracy with 350 different businesses to a burgeoning enterprise focusing on just 17 businesses. As a result, GE's revenues rose to a record $90.84 billion in 1997, a 15 percent increase over the previous year's revenues. More important, its profits rose to $8.2 billion, an increase of 13 percent. Moreover, near the end of 1998, GE's total market value neared a staggering $300 billion!

An interesting question for all leaders would be: how do you teach team above the individual in your workplace? Coach Smith began with defense. This was a constant, easily controlled by consistent effort. What would that be for you?

In my workplace, it would be Sunday morning worship. It is regular and predictable. No matter what, Sunday comes every week. It is the engine that drives everything else in the church. Therefore, we spend much time on the staff making sure we're united in what we're doing on Sunday mornings and why we're doing it. Everyone is committed to excellence. That commitment fosters teamwork. We know that every individual is needed to make Sunday morning work. But we also know that no individual is greater than the whole.

As a Leader, Take the Hits

Another way Coach Smith developed the team concept was his commitment that *we* won games and *he* lost them.

He never demeaned a player in the press, even if it might be justified because of a mistake. He did not want to do anything to disrupt the team. And if a player made a mistake, Coach would assume that somehow he had not properly communicated to that player what he should have done.

As a result, the players felt protected. It fostered trust among us when we knew that, as coach, he was willing to take the hits for the team.

I can't begin to emphasize the need for trust for any team or organization. It can be easily lost and difficult to regain. Gaining trust takes hard work, commitment, perseverance, and loyalty. Donna Wyatt, who leads the initiative for Team Development for the North American Division of the Colgate-Palmolive Company, said this about the "payoff" of trust. "In an environment of trust, people begin to tap into their potential and create outcomes that benefit themselves and their organizations...And it is the extraordinary leader — who is both powerful and vulnerable, trustworthy and trusting — who is the architect and resident of the trusting organization."

The extraordinary trust that existed between Coach Smith and his teams came out of his commitment to lose games and let his players win them. He steadfastly refused to embarrass any of his players at any time. In fact, if we made a terrible mistake in a game, he would always wait to take us out. He did not want the fans to think that he was yanking us because of a mistake. He knew that would embarrass us.

In 1971, my senior year, we had won the regular-season ACC championship. South Carolina was still a part of the conference then and our most bitter rival. We had split two games with them during the regular season. We met in the finals of the ACC Tournament to decide who would represent the ACC in the NCAA Tournament. It was a winner-take-all tournament, the pressure of which no contemporary team knows.

With six seconds to go, we were ahead 51–50. Our 6'11" center was jumping against their 6'3" guard. We thought we had the game won. Coach Smith went over all our assignments in the huddle. Somehow, though, not everyone understood what we were supposed to do. The ball was tipped to the wrong spot. South Carolina scored, and we lost 52–51. We were devastated. For many Tar Heel fans that loss stands out as one of the most disappointing losses in Carolina history.

I was in the game when the tip went awry. For years, I did not even want to talk about the game. It was that painful. Finally, a few years ago, when I was visiting with Coach Smith, my curiosity overcame me. I asked him about that game and if I had done anything wrong to cause the loss. He went over every detail of the play. He showed me what he had been trying to do. Then he said, "I wanted you to be here. But that wasn't your fault. That was my fault. No one was really where I wanted them to be. I accept full responsibility for that loss. I didn't communicate well enough as a coach."

I seriously doubt that it was all Coach Smith's fault. We probably did not listen as closely as we should. But I did find it fascinating that more than 20 years after it happened, he was still protecting his players and the team, still taking full responsibility for the losses. *Players win games. Coaches lose them.* The unity of the team is what is most important!

Recognize Potential and Reward Effort

Another thing Coach Smith did to create the team vision was to recognize potential and reward effort. I believe he was always thinking about next year's team when examining a player's potential. He looked for ways to encourage individuals to become better players and contribute to the team.

Pearce Landry tells an interesting story that illustrates this point. He was a Morehead Scholar, recipient of a very prestigious scholarship awarded to outstanding high school students who show giftedness in academics, athletics, leadership, and service. During his sophomore year at Carolina, he played solely on the junior varsity team.

In February, Carolina played Notre Dame. Coach Wiel, the junior varsity coach, came up to Landry before the game and told him that if the game was a blowout, Coach Smith wanted Landry to dress and earn a few minutes playing with the varsity team. He had played in practice against the varsity, but this was beyond his wildest thoughts.

Sure enough, in the second half, Carolina blew the game open. Landry was sitting in the stands wearing a suit and tie. With about 10 minutes left to play, Coach Wiel turned toward the stands and told Landry to run to the locker room and change. "I sprinted out of the stands and back into the tunnel to the locker room," he said. "The assistant manager handed me a uniform with number fifteen on the back. I slipped it on and got back on the court with about four minutes to play. Finally, with about fifty-five seconds to go, I entered the game. That was my claim to fame that year."

"What was Coach Smith trying to accomplish by putting you in for the last minute of the game?" I asked.

"You know, I think he was trying to say to me that there were good things ahead of me if I kept on working. He was trying to give me a little taste of varsity competition so that in my junior and senior years I might be a good practice player. He was also saying, 'Thanks for helping the varsity in practice.' I simply think he was looking ahead to the next two years."

For his junior year, Landry remained pretty much a practice player. He got to play in one important game against LSU on national television. But he kept working and kept getting better. Then his senior year, Larry Davis transferred, Pat Sullivan blew out his back, and suddenly Landry was the sixth man.

"Then I remembered that game against Notre Dame my sophomore year," he said. "That began to boost my confidence. Had Coach been looking to the future, thinking that I might improve enough to help the team, and he wanted to give my confidence a boost? I think so."

Napoleon once said it amazed him that men were willing to sacrifice their lives in order to have a few medals pinned on their chest.

Recognizing potential and rewarding effort pays off in the corporate boardroom as well as on the basketball court. A good leader sees the potential of workers and how they can develop to help the organization in the future. Are you presently doing this as a leader?

I have learned that the best pool for potential staff people are our interns. Yearly we bring on board young people just out of college or those who have just entered ministry. In 18 years of ministry, our staff has increased from two full-time employees to more than 40. The single best resource has been these interns. When they come on staff, I have a hidden agenda to develop them for future teams. The results have been extraordinary.

We expose the interns to every area of church life. When they show exceptional ability, we find out their primary interest and give that to them as a full-time responsibility. Invariably, they then desire to stay on staff and pour their hearts into this ministry.

Like Coach Smith putting a junior varsity player in for the last minute of a big game, we look for ways to reward our interns by getting them involved in meaningful work and giving them a chance to show their potential. It's a powerful strategy.

John F. Welch Jr. is chairman and CEO of General Electric Company. In his 1995 annual report, he described the leadership challenge of getting everyone in the company involved. He wanted to give GE's 222,000 employees "what the best small companies give people:

voice." To do that, GE came up with a plan called Work-Out. Welch wrote:

> Work-Out was based on the simple belief that people closest to the work know, more than anyone, how it could be done better. It was this enormous reservoir of untapped knowledge, and insight, that we wanted to draw upon. People of disparate ranks and functions search for a better way, every day, gathering in a room for an hour, or three days, grappling with a problem or an opportunity, and dealing with it, usually on the spot — producing real change instead of memos and promises of further study.

While most people think factories should run with machine-like precision, Charlene Pedrolic, the manufacturing chief at Rowe furniture in Salem, Virginia, tore apart the assembly line. She sent gluers, staplers, and seamstresses away and ordered them to build their sofas as they best believed it should happen. The result? Productivity, profit, and employee satisfaction jumped through the ceiling.

Bob Nelson, vice president of Blanchard Training and author of *1001 Ways to Reward Employees*, says one of the primary ways an employer can motivate people today is "to involve employees in decisions, especially when those decisions affect them." It gives them a sense of ownership in their work and the work environment.

That may be the latest advice from the business world, but it's something Coach Smith was doing in college basketball almost 30 years ago. Who made the rules and regulations for each new season? The seniors did. He believed they would know best what the team needed. Because he trusted the seniors to make the rules, they felt more ownership. The other members of the team felt they could give input as well. They felt represented. The team was enhanced.

I personally practice a lot of management by walking around. But I've tried to take this a step further for greater effectiveness. While I'm interacting with staff people, as I find them doing something good and commend them for it, I also regularly ask, "Hey, about this problem in the church, what do you think might be a solution?" Not only have I sometimes received some great solutions, but also the workers regularly feel like they are a part of what's going on.

It's just another way of recognizing potential and rewarding effort.

Know Your Team Members

Another way Coach Smith helped develop the team was by knowing the players and communicating honestly with each member of the team.

In some ways a coach needs to be a master psychologist. He has to try to understand each player's personality, his unique psychological make-up. This information is critical to know in order to make the proper decisions for the team. I experienced Coach's Smith unique ability in this area first-hand.

As shared previously, I worked hard preparing for my senior season. I readily understood that the two players with whom I would be competing were better players: Bill Chamberlain and Dennis Wuycik.

Yet during preseason practice, I outplayed both of them daily. Coach Smith started me the first three games of the season. We won all three, and I was averaging 16 points and eight rebounds per game. The fourth game was against Creighton, a nationally ranked team. I started that game, too, but was taken out after about four minutes; Chamberlain played most of the rest of the game. He played extremely well and we won.

The fifth game saw Chamberlain become the other starting forward, and he remained in that spot for the rest of the season. I started 11 games altogether, filling in when someone was hurt or disciplined. It was a very fulfilling season, although I always wondered why I was moved to the sixth-man role when I clearly outplayed the others in practice.

When I was a graduate assistant at the University of Florida, I summoned the courage to ask Coach John Lotz why this had occurred. He had been an assistant when I played at UNC. I was not bitter, not holding a grudge, I told him. I was simply curious.

Coach Lotz paused for a few moments. Then he finally said, "David, that was a very difficult decision for Coach Smith. You know how he preaches that your game time is related to how you play in practice. But one day he came in and simply said, 'Dave will accept coming off the bench and having a lesser role. It'll be more difficult for Bill to accept since he's such a gifted athlete. Bill will play harder if he's a starter. It will be better for the team if David comes off the bench.' And that was that."

I was not hurt or miffed when Coach Lotz told me how Coach Smith had made the decision. In fact, something deep inside said, "You know, he's right!" It was undoubtedly a good coaching decision, based on the fact that Coach Smith knew the psychological make-up and talent level of his individual players. But his decisions were always made for the betterment of the team. I think he knew I would accept that.

How did Coach Smith get to know his players so well? It started during the recruiting process. James Worthy shared with me how, during Coach Smith's recruitment visit, Coach Smith talked about five minutes to Worthy and then spent most of the evening conversing with his parents. He talked with them about the scholarship, life, and his experiences growing up in Kansas. He spent very little time talking about basketball. At the time it was puzzling to Worthy. "Later in life," Worthy said, "I realized what he had been doing. In getting to know my parents, he was getting to know me. That was the best way he knew of to get to know the recruits."

Leaders, do you know the psychological make-up of your individual team players? There are many tools on the market to help you (i.e. DISC inventory). My entire staff has taken the DISC inventory so we can all understand one another better. Personally, I have found these tools invaluable to understanding my staff, my own make-up — even why sometimes I respond to my wife the way I do! — and the decisions I must make as a leader for the betterment of the team. It has also been very helpful for me to know their family backgrounds. It helps me know them and how they may respond to different situations.

When you understand your team members, then you can develop a relationship with them based on openness and honesty. That's something else I learned from Coach Smith. Not only did he know each player inside and out, but he was always honest with them. It was another way of developing the team.

Regularly, he would cry out in practice, "Know your limits." He would then carefully outline the specific giftedness and limitations of his individual players. Only certain players could shoot three-pointers, or handle the ball on the break. If he didn't think you could do these things, he wouldn't allow you to try. This honesty, accepted as truth because we all wanted what was best for the team, was extremely important.

Before and during the season, Coach Smith would specifically share with each player the role he played. He was honest and plainspoken. At the end of each season, Coach Smith made a personal appointment with each player. He clearly outlined individual strengths and weaknesses. He forthrightly pointed out where they were with the team and how much playing time they would probably receive the next season unless they improved. Then he challenged them to start building on their strengths and improving their weaknesses. Amazingly, he would be so honest that he would even tell a player if he thought he'd never play. Then, if the player concurred and desired to transfer, Coach Smith would help him.

This honesty, I believe, is absolutely crucial to how he developed the team. It helped avoid unnecessary rivalries by clearly defining each player's role on the team. It helped avoid childlike outbursts of "that's not fair!" Each player knew he was appreciated for his own unique contribution to the team.

Some people believe that only positive encouragement and comments should be given to members of the team. They suggest that when a boss sees mistakes in judgment and errors, he should only look for something good to say and not discourage a member of the team with criticism.

Coach Smith would not agree! In practices, during games, and at the end of the season, he would be brutally honest with us. If he had to say something to us in a game, he would always kneel in front of us and quietly talk to us one on one. He was committed to never embarrassing us in front of a crowd. Coach Smith believed that criticism should be given constructively. Moreover, he would give this criticism without favoritism.

Buzz Peterson remembers when Michael Jordan was receiving all the publicity and glamour. "Coach Smith thought it was going to his head. Therefore, from time to time in practice, he would really get on Michael to keep his head level and the team as most important."

Dave Hanners remembers one moment when he experienced Coach Smith's biting tongue. Hanners was a freshman in his very first practice. "It was the first year freshmen were eligible," he said. "He did not want us in the practice in the first place. We all came into the circle at the beginning of practice. It was very sunny outside. I'm from Ohio, and I couldn't believe how bright it was. The light was coming through the windows. I was looking off at the sun, and Coach looked at me. Bang! He got me. He said, 'Dave, what is the emphasis of the day? You seem to know everything and don't need to pay attention. If you don't need to listen, you must already know the emphasis of the day.'

"That put me at a loss. I stuttered. And guess what? I never again looked at anything but Coach when we came to that circle. And I never forgot the emphasis of the day!"

When criticism is thoughtful and sensitively delivered in a timely manner, it can have a positive purpose. Coach *never* scolded, berated, demeaned, or humiliated us. He did become angry at the wrong behavior, but not at us. I think he knew that approval and disapproval are both realities, and it was his job to give both. The way he did it always honored his life principle that we, his players, were his most important products.

When I interviewed Bob Knight, I asked if he thought Coach Smith's greatest strength was loyalty. He said no. Knight thought the better word to describe Coach Smith's greatest asset was *honesty*. "Someone can be loyal to bad things," he said, "but honesty cannot. Honesty is the greatest of all the virtues. Our mutual honesty is what has caused the mutual respect we have for one another."

Coach Smith had this same commitment to honesty with potential recruits. For example, most people thought Kenny Anderson, now with the NBA's New Jersey Nets, would come to Carolina. Many think the reason he didn't come was because of Coach Smith's honesty. Anderson was asking two questions of all the coaches recruiting him. Phil Ford and Coach Smith met with Anderson to try and answer his questions.

The first one from Anderson was, "Coach, will I start as a freshman?" Ford leaned back in his chair, anxious to hear the answer to that one.

Coach Smith responded, "Kenny, if you are as good as people think you are, and if you show the confidence that you have shown at this stage of your career, then the playing time will take care of itself. You don't have to worry about that."

Then came the second question. "Will you let me run the show?" Anderson asked. Ford's back straightened up on that one. He said, "Even I wanted to hear Coach's answer!"

"Kenny," Coach Smith replied, "we have done this for so long I hope you will trust our judgment on matters. My door is always open for discussion. If you have any questions about anything that we do or don't do on the floor, I hope you'll always come in and talk with me about it."

Kenny Anderson went to Georgia Tech. He said he didn't want to be just another horse in Coach Smith's stable. Coach Smith believed the team was greater than the individual. And this principle would not be abrogated, even for a point guard as gifted as Kenny Anderson. Therefore, Coach Smith had to be honest with him, not making any promises during the recruiting process that he couldn't keep later. His honesty may have cost him a talented recruit, but it was best for the team.

Dr. William Schultz, a psychologist who developed strategies to increase productivity with Procter & Gamble and NASA once said that the key for success lies in how well people work together. He went on to say that, in his opinion, the key to people working together is mutual trust and honesty. He concluded, "If people in business just told the truth, eighty percent to ninety percent of their problems would disappear."

It is this principle of honesty that leads to my yearly performance evaluations of my staff. We both clearly understand what's expected of each other. There is open honesty from me to them and, when necessary, from them to me. Actually, I rather enjoy these evaluations. When you have an effective staff, most of the time is spent affirming the great job they are doing and trying to find together how they can do it even better.

Coach Smith taught me the necessity of open candor in leadership.

Create Little Teams on the Big Team

We were playing Georgia Tech in the old Charlotte Coliseum in 1971. We had the better team and were expected to win easily. However, Georgia Tech came out highly motivated, and with 10 minutes left in the first half, we were down by 10.

Dennis Wuycik gave the fist, signaling that he was tired and needed to come out of the game. Coach Smith sent me to the scorer's table. Then Lee Dedmon gave the fist. Craig Corson, the back-up center, followed me to the scorer's table. Then George Karl. Coach Smith was already greatly exasperated with their uninspired play, so he muttered under his breath, "Oh, what the heck!" He told the entire second team to go into the game and replace the first team.

We entered the game with fresh legs and great enthusiasm. Within three minutes we had taken the lead from the Yellow Jackets. Coach Smith then put the starters back into the game. They now had fresh legs and were greatly inspired — and a bit embarrassed! They blew the game wide open.

That game started something that lasted for many years. It was called the Blue Team. This was the second unit that, for most teams, just sits on the bench, watches the games, and serves as cannon fodder for the first team. However, from then on, Coach Smith would regularly substitute the Blue Team in mass force for the first team, with startling results! We almost always held the score until the first team reentered the game, and sometimes we increased the lead.

However, we discovered something much more important than the score. If you give a player a few minutes, even if it's only in the first half when the pressure's not on, he will be ready if you need him in the second half. And, even more important, he will feel that he is a part of the team. After that Georgia Tech game, a new spirit of unity engulfed our team. I'm thoroughly convinced that one of the primary reasons for that team's extraordinary and inexplicable success was the fact that all of us felt we were a part of the team. We believed in Coach Smith's vision for us.

Moreover, the Blue Team had an identity. We even developed our own handshake, one that could only be used by Blue Team members, with our fingers all crunched together as we touched fingertips together. We became highly offended if a player other than a member of the Blue Team used this handshake.

Bill Guthridge, who was then assistant coach, usually coached the Blue Team when we played against the first team. Therefore, we allowed him to use the handshake. In fact, when I visited Coach Guthridge to interview him for this book, he walked out of his office and extended to me the Blue Team handshake — 27 years later!

Thinking back, I realized we had created a team within the team. They were separate teams, yet connected, still with the overall vision of winning together as our goal. We discovered that a team could have smaller teams within the larger team, while still accomplishing the team vision. I remembered how Coach Smith used to break us down into teams of big men and small men to play against each other. Each group developed its own sense of team. When we worked three on three in practice, the vision of teamwork was preached. Coach Smith would sometimes watch preseason three-on-three drills. If he ever saw selfish play, he would find a way to get the message to us.

I do something similar. We have several divisions that oversee the life of the church. We do many things together as a larger staff, activities that promote reciprocal loyalty, create the feel of family, and help us become close friends.

However, as the staff has grown larger, this is increasingly more difficult. Therefore, we try to create smaller teams within the big team. I encourage each division leader to do with their division team what we do as a larger team. They go out for coffee and movies together. They take their own division retreats together. It helps everyone feel like they belong, and the larger team is then made stronger.

Creating little teams within the big team is one of the most important things you can do to promote team unity. And helping every player, or staff member, feel they belong to the team has a snowball effect, building and building on itself with greater and greater results.

The same concept is still working in the Carolina basketball program. And not only has it unified the team, it has spilled over to the fans.

One of the most amazing scenes in the 1997–98 season occurred in the home game against Florida State. UNC may well have played its best game of the season. It was a blowout against a very good Seminoles team. With about 12 seconds left, Scott Williams, the son of Kansas's Roy Williams, was playing during what is known as mop-up time.

The game had obviously been won, but the crowd and the entire team were intensely into the game. Why? Because Williams does not get to play very much and had not scored a basket in his varsity career. Finally, he drove to the basket, threw the ball into the air, and whoosh! In it went. The bench erupted. They acted as if he had just hit the game-winning basket in the national championship. The players, and even the fans, all knew how important every man is to the team.

Justin Kurault experienced this reality of everyone feeling equal and a part of the team, even though he was the team manager. "There is no one person who is bigger than the program," he said. "Coach put us right there in the locker room with the players. We had a locker just like the players. In fact, ours was a little bigger, to store some of the stuff we needed to do our job. We received the same warm-ups to travel in. When the team received pictures at the end of the season, so did we. I was lucky enough to win three ACC Tournaments, and the managers received rings just like the players."

In their book *The Wisdom of Teams*, Jon R. Katzenbach and Douglas K. Smith wrote:

> Teams are not the solution to everyone's current and future organizational needs. They will not solve every problem, enhance every group's results, nor help top management address every performance challenge. Moreover, when misapplied, they can be both wasteful and disruptive. Nonetheless, teams usually do outperform other groups and individuals. They represent one of the best ways to support the broad-based changes necessary for the high-performing organization.

How about your organization? Do people in your workplace have a chance to be involved? Does your lowest-level employee feel like he or she is a part of the team? If not, why not? Ask yourself what you can do to make them feel that they, too, own the vision. When workers feel they have input into key decisions, oversight, and the overall direction, they feel ownership and work harder to make the team's vision a reality.

Show Fairness, Not Favoritism

There is one final thing you can do to develop a team vision, and that is to treat each team member fairly. It's another leadership lesson I learned from Coach Smith.

According to Coach Guthridge, this might be Dean Smith's greatest genius in creating a team. Everyone knew that he treated his players fairly. So how could anyone argue with him if he chose to play one person more than someone else? They knew it was not an arbitrary decision.

How did Coach Smith accomplish this? Guthridge said the major way of ensuring fairness stemmed from the hierarchical system of moving freshmen to seniors. If you were a senior, you knew you would get every opportunity to play, even if a freshman was playing at the same level.

This conviction was at the heart of the struggles of the 1994 team. Four out of five starters returned from the '93 championship team. Three heralded freshmen also came on board. The freshmen were enormously talented. In practice they regularly challenged the incumbents. But the majority of playing time went to the seniors. If it were even, the seniors got the edge.

Eddie Fogler, presently head coach at South Carolina, says this states to the incoming players that you have to pay your dues in the system. It says to the freshmen, "Coming out of high school, you haven't put anything into this system." From day one, people learn that service to the organization has its benefits. And if you pay your dues, you will be rewarded.

Woody Durham, the Tar Heels' radio voice, pointed out an example of this respect for seniors that many people would not know about. Carolina played in the 1977 national championship game against Marquette. Coach Smith was coaching against Al McGuire. They are good friends and had learned much basketball from one another. The game was a chess match, with Carolina finally getting the lead in the second half. Then Coach Smith went into the Four Corners at a crucial point in the game.

Mike O'Koren was a fabulous freshman who had 34 points in the semi-final game against UNLV. He gave the tired signal and exited the game right before Carolina gained the lead. Bruce Buckley, now a prominent Charlotte attorney, took his place.

When Carolina regained the lead, Eddie Fogler leaned across Bill Guthridge and said to Coach Smith, "Don't you think we should take a time-out and get Mike back in the game?"

"Now think about this," Durham continued. "It's the national championship game. Coach Smith had been to three Final Fours in the late 1960s. He had taken another team to the Final Four in 1972. Comments were spreading nationally that perhaps Dean Smith was not a great coach because he couldn't win the supposed big one. Do you know how he responded to Eddie? He said he would never embarrass a senior like Bruce Buckley by taking him out of the game like that.

"Right after that, Bruce had a shot blocked and the momentum of the game changed a bit. That's not to say Carolina lost the game because of this decision. It is to say that Coach Smith was concerned with how his seniors were cared for, concerned with his loyalty to them, even in a national championship game!"

Freshmen don't like this hierarchy, nor do they understand it. But it's birthed in the conviction that this is the fair thing to do. It's best for the team. When you become a junior or senior, you especially appreciate it. And the team is more unified. It states in a subtle but loud way, "The team is more important than the individual."

For this book I asked Coach Smith if he had any regrets about how he taught team basketball. Would he change anything in the way he coached?

His answer was intriguing. "I don't think I delegated enough to my assistants. I always valued input from the players, but I probably didn't receive enough from the assistants. I love the way Coach Guthridge is doing it now. They have a three-hour staff meeting every morning to talk everything over. Everybody has ideas. Everybody has input.

"I used to have the practice plan and then spend about an hour talking about practice. I would say, 'Here is what we are going to do' instead of saying, 'What do you think?' I think I controlled too much. I knew I had a vision of how I thought a team should play and how to bring that about. But if I were coaching today, I'd probably allow more input from the assistants. They have good ideas too."

He may well be stating the obvious paradigm shift in leadership that has occurred during the last decade. In the 1970s and 1980s, the autocratic leadership style was still honored. The general was the general, and if he thought the hill should be taken, he simply ordered it and the underlings obeyed. Now, in the 1990s, many people feel qualified, educated, and competent. Those who are second or third in command simply find it difficult to obey the top person if they think there may be a better way to reach the goal.

Nowhere is this better illustrated than the movie *Crimson Tide*. The commander, played by Gene Hackman, received the command to fire nuclear weapons on Russia. However, one checkpoint was missing. The second in command, played by Denzel Washington, fearful of a nuclear holocaust and confident of his own leadership ability, took command of the ship. He wasn't sure the commander was right. He demanded input.

The movie is a thrilling example of the leadership shift from the 1980s to the 1990s. Who was right? In a way, Gene Hackman was right, because every organization, especially the military, needs firm leadership, a person in control with authority and a vision. Yet, in another way, Denzel Washington was right, because competent assistants can and should give input. Their input could avert disaster, as the movie clearly teaches.

This shift in leadership style is largely attributable to Baby Boomers entering their forties. We're well-educated, independent, entrepreneurial, and were reared to question authority, even when authority is ours.

It's this shift that I think Coach Smith senses. If he still coached today, I'm sure he would make that shift easily and ably. And the team would still be the vision, and he would still be successful.

Coach Smith said to me, "Our philosophy, as you know, has been simple: play hard, play smart, and, most important, play together. And I don't think any player, five years after he has left this program has ever regretted coming here."

When people play for a coach whose vision is the team over the individual, they are learning something much larger and more important than playing basketball. They learn how to live and play together, how to get along with one another, how to be independent yet interdependent, how to be a team, how to live life as it's supposed to be lived.

At Carolina we believed in Coach's vision that teams, not individuals, win games. Dean Smith convinced us of this truth. We bought it. We lived it.

And it's difficult to argue with his success.

Thought for the Day

**The vision of the team is more important
than the individuals on the team.**

Game Plan

- Teach what's important in the vision

- As the leader, take the hits

- Recognize potential and reward effort

- Know your team members

- Create little teams on the big team

- Show fairness, not favoritism

Team Practice

- How important is teamwork to the success of your organization?

- What actions are you taking to build a strong team?

- How do you reward individual effort so that it
contributes to team results?

SUCCESS REQUIRES
A FLEXIBLE VISION

*"We don't have a system,
but a philosophy that is
flexible and innovates."*

It rankles Coach Smith whenever his vision is called a system. "'To me,'" he said, "that connotes that we're rigid, that we don't change with our personnel, and that's just not true. Now if you say North Carolina has a philosophy, I love that. We change every year, even though the basic vision remains the same."

He was a stickler for fundamentals, emphasizing them over and over. The approach might change, but the fundamentals stayed the same from year to year.

For example, in 1971, my senior year, Coach Smith knew we were predicted to finish at the bottom of the conference. So, on the first day of practice, he called us to the middle of the court. He held a basketball in his hands. He looked at all of us and said, "Gentlemen, this is a basketball." Then we began drills on dribbling, passing, rebounding, and shooting. They were drills we had done in junior high school. But Coach Smith knew that for us to be a good team, he had to reemphasize the fundamentals.

Every company, corporation, or church that is accomplishing anything of note has core values and fundamentals. And those basic elements need to be repeated, relearned, and reemphasized regularly, at least yearly. I contend that no innovation takes place outside of a commitment to these fundamentals. During his 36 years of coaching, every one of Coach Smith's teams had these fundamentals as a foundation.

I take every opportunity I can to return to Chapel Hill and reminisce about four of the happiest years in my life. So in 1993, the year Coach Smith won his second NCAA championship, it was a "no brainer" when I was invited to speak to a Christian organization on the UNC campus.

I decided to make it an event. I called the basketball office and got permission to observe practice. I then asked my six-year-old daughter, Bethany, if she would like to accompany me to my old college stomping grounds. She eagerly agreed, especially when she found out it would take her out of school a few hours early.

Speaking to several hundred students at the campus event was exhilarating. Bethany and I walked around the university and had dinner at "The Rat," a UNC institution. It brought back special memories that I excitedly shared with her. However, the highlight of the trip was the privilege of viewing practice.

We entered the Smith Center almost in a hushed, reverent awe. I shared with Bethany how this was going to be a new experience for me, too, since I had played in Carmichael Auditorium. This was my first practice in the Smith Center. As we settled in our seats, I looked forward to seeing how practice might be different some 20 years later.

You can therefore imagine my deep introspection as the next two hours unfolded in remarkable similarity to the many practices I had personally experienced years earlier. Practice began with a huddle at center court and a player reciting the thought for the day. Then came the drills to enhance the fundamentals. The drills were precise and exactly timed. The emphasis was on teamwork and unselfish play.

The thought for the day was repeated over and over. All of it struck a familiar chord.

Coaches Smith and Guthridge constantly adjured the players to listen to what they said and respond immediately and accordingly. More and more I felt a sense of déjà vu, that I was reliving a part of my past.

Teach the Fundamentals

For the next two hours, I heard Coach Smith say things I had heard more than 20 years earlier, phrases that emphasized the fundamentals of his understanding of how the game should be played. No wonder these things had become the foundation of the concepts I have used in my own leadership.

Let me give you a few familiar examples of things I heard during the practice session.

"You play like you practice." Over and over again I have stated to my staff that the one-time event is fine, but the best results are produced as a result of a day-in and day-out commitment to work.

"Little things win games." The big shot may get headlines at the end of the game, but equally important are the little things that set up the victory. When every member of the team, both on the bench and in the game, consistently practices the fundamentals for 40 straight minutes, it allows a person to take the big shot and score the win. How often I tell my staff, "The details do matter." If a company is successful only 98 percent of the time, the profit loss could be in the millions!

"Keep trying! Good things happen when you play hard." Surely this attitude, planted in practice, is the reason for the dozens of miracle comebacks engineered by Coach Smith throughout the years. In the huddle during a close game, he often turned to different players and emphasized this reality. "Just keep at it. Keep playing hard."

In the Eastern Regional final against Louisville in 1997, the Tar Heels watched a 20-point lead melt to three with about eight minutes to go. Coach Smith called the team together during a time-out and said, "This has been a great season. We've had a great run. Thank you for all your hard work."

The players were confused. They looked at one another. Was Coach Smith giving up?

Finally, Ademola Okulaja shouted out, "No! It's not over!"

Coach Smith looked at the rest of the team and asked, "Do you all agree?"

"Yes!"

Then he designed a play to score out of the huddle. They scored. It stopped the Louisville run and the lead was quickly built back to double digits. They coasted to a win and went to the Final Four.

"Being in shape doesn't mean you'll never get tired. It means you'll recover more quickly." In my opinion, this is a great fundamental of life to teach to those who work with us and under us. We all become tired in our work. We then feel guilty for being tired, thinking no one else ever tires. Fatigue is a reality, but we know we're healthy when we recover from it quickly.

Coach Smith always believed that the sign of being in good shape was not if a player became tired, but how quickly he recovered after becoming tired. If the recovery period wasn't fast enough, it signaled to him that we needed more conditioning.

If a person doesn't recover quickly from a mistake, that's a sure signal to us as leaders that they need more conditioning, more training. Continual mistakes may be the fault of the boss, not the worker!

"Freshmen, go get the ball!" Any time a ball rolled away, a freshman was expected to spring to it and bring it back. From the beginning of their very first practice, the freshmen, no matter how exceptionally talented or highly recruited they may be, were expected to serve the upperclassmen.

I wonder how leaders are today about teaching employees the value of serving and also of waiting for rewards. I've learned through the years that the best staff people are those who have first learned their own unimportance and are willing to give themselves to others for the sake of the vision and the team. The top staff people also have not fallen prey to the American lie of instant gratification. They are willing to work hard, persevere, and wait for the rewards.

A tug on my sleeve interrupted my musings during the basketball practice. Bethany had been watching Coach Smith run practice for quite some time. "Daddy," she said, "I like him. He's like my first-grade teacher, Mrs. Davis. Kind, but firm." I laughed inwardly. A child has the ability to see the truth very clearly and easily. She was exactly on target.

Coach Smith is firm on his commitment to the fundamentals that guide his team. These fundamentals are immutable. After 879 wins, it's easy to see how successful the annual teaching of these fundamentals can become.

In the church I pastor, our leadership team has worked hard to define six fundamental, core values. We regularly go over them together and with our church. We practice them over and over again. We are convinced that they are the foundation for the success of this church.

Why is teaching the fundamentals so important to success? Here's an illustration from 1970.

Charlie Scott, UNC's All-American guard, could do things with a basketball that would amaze people even today. He was a superb athlete with unbelievable ball-handling skills. One day in practice, he came down court and completed an amazing behind-the back, no-look pass that led to a basket. All the players paused and applauded the pass.

What was Coach Smith's response? He said, "Charles, the great player is the one who makes the hard play look easy, not the easy play look hard."

Coach Smith was simply restating his conviction that fundamentals, properly performed within the team, win games, not spectacular, individual plays.

Innovate as Necessary

But the fundamentals are also the foundation for innovation. And, in fact, unless these fundamentals have regular, even annual, innovations, they will not work.

The fundamentals of dribbling, passing, shooting defense, and rebounding represented Coach Smith's philosophy. But it was a flexible philosophy, and his innovations, that kept each team fresh and effective each individual season. A part of Coach Smith's genius is that he did innovate and change when necessary to accommodate his personnel.

Pearce Landry told me this story about Coach Smith's willingness to be creative. In 1995 Carolina was the number-one team in the nation. They had experienced only one loss. "We were about halfway through the ACC season and we came off just a horrible performance against Notre Dame. I can't remember the team. We ended up winning, but it was a team we should have beaten by twenty.

"We showed up at practice the next day and found out Coach had suddenly changed our whole defensive scheme. He told us we weren't going to run what we had been running to that point. He said we simply didn't have the personnel to do what we're doing. He knew that if we were going to be successful in the NCAA tournament, we didn't have the horses to play that kind of defense. So he switched to a more passive defense that put pressure on the three-point shooter. We ended up going to the Final Four."

Most very successful corporations know the value of innovation. Johnson and Johnson encourages new innovations and personal initiative. Then the successful experiments that are profitable and fit the company's core ideology are retained. They encourage multiple attempts at innovation and are unafraid of failure. They feel innovation and failure are twin sisters.

How important is it in business for a leader to have foundations that remain flexible enough for innovation? Peter Drucker once predicted failure within four years for any leading corporation that loses its proactivity.

Over and over again, in the history of corporate management, his thesis has proven to be correct. Fully half of the Fortune 500 companies between 1975 and 1980 no longer exist. Drucker has updated his prediction. He now believes it takes only 18 months to go from leader to loser. Even failure runs the risk of downsizing today!

Imparato and Harari give a startling insight into this leadership secret in their classic book, *Jumping the Curve*. After interviewing CEOs of various companies that averaged 15 times better than the Dow during the past 20 years, they concluded that the biggest threat to a company's survival is complacency. The refusal to be innovative is a terminal disease for corporate America.

Peter Drucker points out how the Japanese and Koreans are organizing innovation. "They've set up small groups of their brightest people to systematically apply the discipline of innovation to identify and develop new business. Innovation requires us to systemically identify changes…to abandon rather than defend yesterday — something most difficult for existing companies to do."

Converse was the shoe I wore in high school and college. I can still describe in detail what this canvas shoe looked like. Chuck Taylor's name was printed on the shoe. Everyone, and I mean everyone, wore their Chucks, as we all called them. It was the elite shoe for basketball players.

Here's a simple question: What happened to Converse? In the '80s and '90s Nike, Reebok, and other shoe magnates have left them in the dust. Converse had a great shoe for the '60s and '70s. But it failed to innovate. It is just now coming back with a contemporary canvas Chuck. But the failure to innovate left Converse in the back of the pack with a long way to catch up.

IBM once dominated the computer market but became complacent. Microsoft and other companies read the future more accurately, innovating and passing IBM, which then had to reorganize completely to try and catch up. If innovation does not happen regularly, the game will pass you by.

Twenty years ago, one bought hamburgers at a hamburger restaurant. McDonald's ruled. Then other fast-food chains started to innovate. They realized people wanted more choices — some for health reasons, others for more diversity in menu selections. Today practically all the franchises offer baked potatoes, chicken, salads, and Mexican options. Those who did not innovate were left behind.

Bank of America in Charlotte, North Carolina, has grown and merged with several banks across the country to become the second largest bank in America. Yet it has also been on the cutting edge of new innovations that have allowed continuing growth. For example, Bank of America placed ATM machines in as many places as possible. Recently, however, it began to see that more and more people wanted to transact business from their homes. Therefore, Bank of America went on the cutting edge of online banking and has led the way in this enterprise. If it hadn't, Bank of America would have been left behind.

American Airlines foresaw a way of encouraging more customers to fly their airline: frequent flyer miles. The company began awarding customers travel points when they flew American. More and more travelers saw the potential benefits and chose American. Now every airline offers this innovation.

Charles Schwab saw the potential of eliminating the middle-man for individual investors. A huge company was built on an innovation: bypassing the investment broker with a direct phone call to Schwab, with the additional savings passed on to customers.

Innovation is necessary for churches, too. Several hundred churches close every year. As pastors, many of us knew that something had to be done or America would become like postmodern Europe, with beautiful, but empty, cathedrals everywhere.

About six years ago I changed the vision of the church I lead. Previously, we had a vision of basically taking care of our own. That is certainly necessary; but unless the church is directed outward, it will die. We therefore transitioned ourselves to a more current, progressive church. We initiated contemporary music, drama, and other methodologies to reach people who were bored with church or thought it to be irrelevant.

This change in vision was one of the most difficult times in my ministry, an episode that I will share in more depth when I get to the topic of dealing with failure. During this period I received more criticism than ever before. My wife, Marilynn, helped by remarking that whenever anything new is born, it must go through a time of transition. She reminded me that in childbirth the most painful stage of labor is the final one, called transition, which occurs just before delivery. This is the time when the wife may say to her husband, "You're the reason this happened to me. I hate you!" She doesn't really mean it, but the pain during this transition time is unbearable.

People in the church were undergoing a painful time of transition. Did it finally stop? Yes, it did. Are we in a much better position now? Indeed we are.

The new vision is working. The innovation was necessary. We're now a church ready to face the twenty-first century!

Change is Constant

It's easy to keep on doing something that is successful and remain unwilling to change. But courageous leaders are unwilling to say, "If it ain't broke, don't fix it." They know they constantly need to break something in order to make it better, in order to reach even higher objectives.

Consider that, right now, we know only three percent of all the information that will be available to us by the year 2010. The world around us is constantly changing. The attitudes of Generation X and the following generation, the Millennials, are different from Boomers. We had better be willing to understand them — willing to innovate and change — or leaders and organizations will be left behind.

The contemporary market place leaves leaders no choice except to embrace innovation and change. Change will arrive monthly in tsunami-like proportions and will threaten to eradicate organizations overnight. Therefore, today's leaders will only be able to survive by encouraging their people, their most important asset, to act immediately on their knowledge and beliefs.

Wayne Gretzky, perhaps the world's best hockey player, said it this way: "You miss one hundred percent of the shots you never take."

Stephen Covey, in his book *Principle-Centered Leadership,* says, "A strategic leader can provide direction and vision, motivate through love, and build a complementary team based on mutual respect if he is more ...concerned with direction and results than with methods, systems, and procedures. While all of the producers are hacking their way through the jungle and their managers are sharpening their machetes for them and setting up machete-wielding working schedules and putting on training programs for machete wielders, an enlightened and courageous leader must sometimes cry out, 'Wrong jungle!' even though he can expect to receive the answer, 'Be quiet! We're making progress.'"

Coach Smith was annually willing to wail, "Wrong jungle!" He was always willing to innovate, to make his vision stronger with new concepts and ideas. Some of his innovations are now legendary. Coaches at every conceivable level now institute these different concepts to foster team play. Let me give you a few examples.

Thank Those Who Assist

The player who scores the point must point to the player who gave him the pass. Everyone recognizes the scorer; Coach Smith wanted to make sure all the spectators knew who gave the pass, because scoring two points was impossible without the pass. If someone failed to point, and Coach Smith noticed it while reviewing game films, the entire team would have to run extra sprints the next day in practice. When one player fails, the entire team is hurt, not just the individual.

Bobby Jones, the All-American forward in the 1970s, once missed a lay-up in a game. He still pointed to the person who gave him the pass. Coach Smith liked that. The next day it was instituted in practice. Now hundreds of teams, from youth leagues to the professional teams, do the same — whether the basket is scored or not.

Coach Smith was trying to teach us about life by learning to point to the person who gave us the pass, the person who made it possible to score. No great leader has ever reached any position of significant success without saying thanks to those who have helped him achieve it.

After win number 878 Dean Smith did not take time to bask in the glory of tying Coach Rupp's record; he was too busy thanking his former players. A national television audience watched him traverse the tunnel to the locker room, stopping every few feet to shake hands and greet the scores of players who had come from all over just to be there for the momentous occasion. By his actions Coach Smith was saying that we were the ones who had allowed him to achieve this success.

Was he sincere? I am absolutely convinced of it. Long before win number 879 ever came, he annually wrote all his former players and their families at Christmas, often thanking us for our friendship and what we have meant to him through the years. He would ask us to say hello to our wives, kids, and parents. This letter would accompany the media guide. I've received one every year since graduation in 1971. I had been in Ostend, Belgium, less than a month, beginning my first year with the European professional leagues, when I received a letter from Coach Smith thanking me for the four years I played for him.

Hearing the simple words *thank you* can have a powerful effect on employees as well as basketball players. Max Depree, in his wonderful little book *Leadership is an Art,* wrote, "What is it most of us really want from work? We would like to find the most effective, most productive, most rewarding way of working together. ...We would like a work process and relationships that meet our personal needs for belonging, for contributing, for meaningful work, for the opportunity to make a commitment, for the opportunity to grow and be at least reasonably in control of our own destinies. Finally, we'd like someone to say, 'Thank you.'"

Depree contends that effective leadership today cannot be leadership by control, but leadership by persuasion. One of the ways, he says, that people feel they are participating in the process is when the leader simply says, "Thanks."

A raise is not always the best way for a boss to say, "Well done." Most often workers want a simple "thank you," personally stated or on paper. Bob Nelson, who wrote *1001 Ways to Energize People,* said, "Raises are expected. Their value has been diminished." He goes on to say that employee validation does not have to be elaborate or expensive. E-mail or voice mail, or a verbal affirmation in a staff meeting can suffice. In a newspaper interview Nelson added, "If you think you're too busy to do this kind of thing, you need to reassess your priorities. Most people don't worry about their people until they're walking out the door. By then it's too late. Do it now! Don't wait until the annual banquet!"

Monthly I ask my program staff to submit names to me of people in their ministries who are doing outstanding work. I then sit down and write each one a thank-you card, specifically noting what they have done.

The recipient of one of those cards sticks in my mind. Grace, a 70-something-year-old grandmother who tirelessly works in our kitchen, came up to me one Wednesday night at our community meal. She had ketchup stains all over her apron. Her shoulders were a bit hunched over. She was obviously tired from her duty of serving food and clearing the tables. Yet as she approached me, she had a gleam in her eye. For the next few moments she effusively thanked me for sending her a thank-you note. She was overwhelmed that I would take time from my busy schedule to write her. And I'll never forget the last thing she said to me. "You know, David, I'm going to work even harder now."

In a recent staff meeting, I had just come from another meeting where someone outside my church profusely praised my youth pastor. Before the entire staff, I repeated what I heard. Fischer's face lit up! The next day he came to my office door to thank me for publicly thanking him.

Everyone likes for someone to say, "Thank you for the pass."

Help Those Who Sacrifice

Here's another one of Coach Smith's innovations that other coaches have adopted. When a player dived on the floor for a loose ball, the player closest to him had to run and help him up. One had sacrificed for the team. Therefore, another team member ought to come to his aid. If someone failed to do this, the entire team would have to run the next day in practice.

I constantly look for the person on my staff who is diving for the ball, that person who is going over and above the call of duty, who is willing to move outside his or her own area of responsibility to help someone else who is overwhelmed. When I see this kind of sacrifice, I love to reward it with a meal out, or movie passes, or a half-day off — anything that communicates that a sacrifice for the sake of the team will be properly rewarded.

We even have a Giant-killer Award, a statue of David slaying Goliath, for the one who tackles a difficult problem and finds a solution. The recipient gets to keep the statue in his or her office until the next giant arises. They also receive another small benefit, such as a meal out or time off.

Stand Up and Cheer

When a player came out of the game, those on the bench had to stand up and cheer for him. Yes, sometimes this action felt coerced and contrived (take it from someone who had to do it practically his entire sophomore year!), but Coach Smith believed good little habits develop into good big habits. He also wanted us to be in the game just in case he called upon us to play. So we did what he told us to do. Plus, it didn't hurt to know that as he watched game films he would always notice if someone didn't stand up. And if we didn't stand up, the entire team would run the next day.

But I think he was trying to accomplish something greater. I believe he was creating synergy, the power of encouragement, within a team.

I do something similar occasionally with my staff. I'll gather all of us together and then put a chair in the middle of the room. Each person on the staff must sit in the chair for two minutes. They cannot say a thing. Then everyone else fills in the blank about the person sitting in the middle of the room. "I like you because... "

Yes, the person in the chair can be a bit embarrassed. But they really feel good about themselves! Everyone develops an attitude of encouragement. It's like, well, like applauding when someone comes off the court. It creates team spirit, and staff people love it.

Give Them a Chance to Rest

If someone became tired during the game, he stuck his fist in the air and asked to come out. If a player took himself out of a game, he could then put himself back in when he was rested. Coach Smith adamantly believed that a rested reserve would perform better than a tired superstar. The team must be considered first!

Many Carolina fans gasped during the 1993 NCAA championship game against Michigan, when Coach Smith inserted seldom used point guard Scott Cherry into a closely contested game after the starting point guard, Derrick Phelps, had given the tired signal with a little more than six minutes left. Cherry only played a minute, but he played admirably without making a mistake. Phelps got his rest, re-entered the game for the stretch drive, and finished the game brilliantly.

Yes, Carolina won the game. Coach Smith simply knows that fatigue makes cowards of us all. He would not let fatigue be a factor in whether a game is won or lost. He let us make the decision to come out of the game when tired. Otherwise, the only reason he would ever take us out of a game was for lack of effort, not fatigue.

I don't hesitate to tell workers who seem tired to leave and go get some rest or do something fun. The job still gets done, most often better than if I had forced them to work continuously in their fatigue. That's why I carefully monitor if my staff is taking their weekly day off. It's partly to help them build their own families on a firm foundation. And it's a lot cheaper than paying a huge family-counseling bill! But it's also the realization that rested reserves play better than tired superstars. Proper rest determines job performance.

Let Innovation Flow from the Vision

When I asked Coach Smith if he had carefully planned out all these innovations, he laughed. "Not a one." He noticed my surprise and said, "David, I really didn't plan these things. They all just kind of happened. I was simply living by my conviction of the team being above the individual player. Then, as I lived by this principle, these innovations simply occurred."

Isn't his answer interesting? He did not spend hours trying to think about the innovations for which he is famous. He was simply living by his life principles — in this case, the principle that the team is what's most important — and the innovations simply fell into place.

Too often, I think, leaders do just the opposite. We spend countless hours trying to be creative. Yet with Coach Smith, the creativity flowed spontaneously out of a commitment to live by certain principles and core values.

As corporate structures and cultures have been downsized and work forces slashed, as lackluster performance in revenue growth occurs, some leaders have built a culture of cynicism and despair. As a result, they have lost their most important resource: human capital. Perhaps the answer is not pushing our people to work harder, but to ask the question, "Is the team our highest priority? Does this guide everything we do?"

If we emphasized this, perhaps the creativity and innovation that are necessary for any organization to succeed would flow more easily from our work associates.

Thought for the Day

Develop a philosophy, not a system.

Game Plan

- Teach the fundamentals
- Innovate as necessary
- Understand that change is constant
- Let innovation flow from the vision

Team Practice

- To what degree do you seek new solutions to problems?
- How do you prepare for change?
- How do you encourage others to innovate?
- What can your organization do to encourage innovation?

AS INDIVIDUALS IMPROVE, THE TEAM IMPROVES

"If you want to make the team better, become a better individual player."

B etween my sophomore and junior years at UNC, I made the decision not to transfer. I wanted to see if I could play in the ACC and particularly at North Carolina. But my personal aspirations had melted away; I primarily wanted to help the team be the best it could be. So I called Coach Smith and told him I was committed to staying at North Carolina.

"How can I best help the team?" I asked him.

"If you want to help the team," he said, "become a better individual player." He then reemphasized my weaknesses and strengths. He told me to work on both, become a better player, and the team would be better.

At first glance, you might think Coach Smith's statement contradicts his vision of the team being above the individual. On the contrary, it only enhances it. A team is made up of individual parts. It is the leader's job to take the unique giftedness of different individuals and mold them together as a team with a common vision and goal. The stronger, the more gifted those individual parts are, the stronger the team's potential.

I worked hard that summer to become a better player. Often in the hot sun of Orlando, Florida, as I ran sprints and lifted weights, I asked myself, "Why am I doing this?" I would always pant the answer, "Because this is making the team better."

Dave Hanners posed an interesting question when I interviewed him for this book. "Can you name one North Carolina player who didn't get better between his freshman and senior seasons?" he asked. He couldn't think of one, and either could I. Coach Smith had to deal with all our egos, trying not to bruise them, yet getting the best out of us for the sake of the team. "Most coaches can't do that," Hanners said. "They usually fail somewhere."

Coach Smith also mused with me about how much better some players became during their careers, even to his amazement. "Darrell Elston came here because John Lotz knew his high school coach," he told me. "Darrell had a basketball scholarship from Ball State and a football scholarship from Purdue. He was the fourteenth man on the squad in 1972. In the Final Four, he couldn't even dress for the game because the rules stated that only twelve players could dress. I told Darrell that perhaps he should go some place else where he could play. But he worked hard over the years and became an all-ACC performer. He worked very hard, and the team became better."

A great leader can motivate others toward self-discipline and personal responsibility. No matter how gifted the player may be, or how much playing time he may receive, Coach Smith believed that the individual — whether the manager, a bench player, a regular, or a superstar — can have tremendous impact on the team when he personally improves.

Teach Personal Responsibility and Self-Discipline

A jar rests on the corner of Coach Guthridge's desk. It's an "excuse" jar. When you come in to see him, the first thing you're expected to do is file your excuses in the jar. He simply won't listen to them. Every player on the team is constantly challenged to assume personal responsibility for becoming a better player. He knows it will make the team better. I'm certain that he learned this from Coach Smith.

I am one of the three chaplains to the NBA's Charlotte Hornets. Before the games I lead a 15-minute chapel service to remind the six or so players who attend about the true source of all their gifts. It's a time of reflection, a time to remember what's really important and who is really in control of all things.

The first time I led the service, I wanted to capture their attention. So I opened with a question. "Who is the toughest player you've ever tried to guard?"

George Zidek immediately said, "Hakeem Olajuwon."

Dell Curry didn't hesitate. "Number 23." (For you non-basketball enthusiasts, that is Michael Jordan's number.)

Anthony Mason just smiled. He wouldn't give an answer. I kept pressing him to give me a name. Finally, he said, "David, there's no one I can't stop!" Everyone laughed, for that's what Mason really believes!

I then told them about trying to guard Julius Erving in the NIT finals my senior year, and how he was unquestionably the most difficult opponent I had ever faced.

"But you know who is the toughest opponent you'll ever have to overcome in your life?" I then asked. "Yourself."

In the lives of all great people, the first victory they ever have to win is over themselves. If we could kick the person in the backside who is most responsible for our problems, we would not be able to sit down for a week.

Winston Churchill once said, "The price of greatness is responsibility."

William Faulkner said, "Don't bother just to be better than your contemporaries or predecessors. Try to be better than yourself."

Coach Smith taught this principle of personal responsibility in several ways. How? First, he demanded self-discipline. He truly believed that the self-disciplined person is a free person.

At every opportunity, he emphasized personal responsibility and self-discipline. I vividly remember a practice on Thanksgiving Day my sophomore year. We were a very good team, ranked number-two in the country during the preseason. Our best player was a very gifted junior named Charlie Scott. He could out-run, out-jump, and out-play anyone else on the team. His athleticism was wondrous.

However, in practice that particular day, Scott was not working very hard. Coach Smith stopped practice. As was his custom, he put us all on the end line. He used one of his famous lines on us: "When one of you doesn't hustle, the whole team suffers. We're going to run for Charles's laziness."

So we ran. Scott, however, refused to run very hard. Everyone knew that in a pure sprint Scott would beat the rest of us by a good 10 feet. But he simply coasted in the middle of the pack.

"We're going to keep running," Coach Smith said, "until Charles runs one sprint as fast as he can."

He blew the whistle and we started to run again ... and again ... and again. Scott refused to run one hard sprint, and Coach Smith refused to budge from his command. The immovable object had met the irresistible force! So we kept on running.

We must have run for an hour or more, over and over and over again. Finally, Rusty Clark, our 250-pound center, walked over to Scott and said, "If you don't run one sprint real hard, we're all going to kill you."

That seemed to be sufficient motivation, and Scott finally ran one sprint as fast as he could. Coach Smith blew his whistle and sent us to the showers with a final instruction, "Be back at three this afternoon so we can cover what we missed this morning."

Another way Coach Smith taught self-discipline was by insisting on punctuality. He knew that simple things like punctuality can turn out to be extremely important. So we had an iron-clad rule: if you're one minute late for the bus, it leaves without you. It didn't matter if you were a sub or superstar, the bus would leave you. If you were late for a pre-game meal, you wouldn't start.

To this day, Bill Chamberlain worries that he may have lost the 1972 national championship for UNC. He was scheduled to be a starter, but was late for the pre-game meal before the Florida State game in the national semifinals. Florida State jumped off to a huge lead and UNC never recovered. We lost by four. Chamberlain wonders if his lack of punctuality disrupted team unity and caused a very important loss.

During my senior year, I had my own narrow escape with Coach Smith's insistence on punctuality. I had finally landed a date with a particular girl and decided to impress her by taking her to the Duke–

Carolina game. Both teams were nationally ranked and it promised to be a good match. Although I wasn't a starter, I was the sixth man and knew I would receive significant playing time.

We were supposed to be at Carmichael Auditorium by 6:30 for an 8:00 televised game. I planned to pick my date up at 6:00, to be sure I'd be on time.

I arrived at her sorority house at the appointed hour and let her know I was downstairs. Five, 10, 15 minutes passed. I began to panic. She finally came downstairs, strutting into the parlor as if every clock worldwide had ceased ticking.

I rushed her to the car and sped over to Carmichael, arriving 15 minutes late. I gave my date a ticket and sprinted to what we called "the cage" to pick up my uniform. Just as I headed toward the door, Coach Smith entered.

"Are you just now arriving?" he asked, studying my face intently.

"N-no," I stammered, "I was just sitting down, reflecting on the game."

He waited a moment and then nodded me toward the locker room.

I quickly dressed and sat breathlessly waiting for his arrival for the pre-game talk. I was certain I had just gone from sixth to tenth man on the team.

Coach Smith always commenced the pre-game meeting by writing the opposing team's starting five players on the board with their numbers next to them. Then he would write our starting five next to the player we would be guarding.

He walked to the board and listed the guards, then the forwards. Next to Duke's all-ACC center he listed my name! Our starting center, unbeknownst to me, had been late to practice the previous day. If you are late to practice, you don't start the next game.

I was so unnerved by my tardy escapade and my run-in with Coach Smith, it did not immediately sink in that I was slated to start against Duke in Carmichael Auditorium — and that I would be guarding Duke's all-conference 6'11" center.

That was probably the best thing that could have happened to me. I didn't have time to think about it, and I went out and hit the first three shots of the game. In fact, I ended up playing one of the best games of my career, with 19 points, seven rebounds, and five assists. We won 79–74.

Did Coach Smith know I really had been late? I never asked. Hopefully, he has a blessed case of amnesia to this day. Or, perhaps, knowing our center was not going to start, he couldn't dare bench me too.

Regardless, I was never late again. To this day I remember how fortunate I was, and what the consequences of tardiness could be.

Use an Inside-Out Approach

The individual is key for total quality to occur on a team. The leader must have this perspective. But Coach Smith saw this truth as an inside-out approach to management, so different from the way many organizations operate. They think that a new system or organization is the answer to productivity.

Management guru Stephen Covey wrote, "There must be individual growth, change, and development to make organizational development and change viable. And yet, as I see it, that basic fact is largely ignored. Too many executives think of change in terms of some outside force acting on internal people and conditions. But fundamentally, change that results in productivity requires an inside-out approach, not an outside-in approach."

Coach Smith used this inside-out approach to teach personal responsibility and self-discipline, and he did it with a very minimum of rules and regulations. That may seem strange. Too many of us tend to think that the more rules and regulations, the more disciplined someone will be. Coach Smith did not adopt this perspective.

Previously, I noted how the seniors annually made the rules for the following season. This action not only allowed tremendous buy-in by the players, but it also allowed those who most closely knew the individual personality of the team to make the rules.

When I visited with Coach Smith, he reminded me that he really only had one rule: don't ever embarrass me, yourself, or the team. Of course, he was the one who judged if that rule were ever broken. But, evidently, it is the one major rule he always had.

I vividly remember when I ran up against the "never embarrass me or the team" rule. It was my sophomore year, when I didn't get to play much. You can therefore imagine my surprise and excitement when Coach Smith touched me on the shoulder in the middle of a significant game and told me to enter. I tore off my sweats and ran to the scorer's bench. Play stopped and I entered the game. Here was my chance to make a positive impression. Here was my long-awaited opportunity to prove I could play at this level.

The ball came to me at the top of the key. No one guarded me. I glanced at the basket and let the ball fly. *Clank!* It bounced off the rim.

Before I knew it, the horn sounded and someone entered the game for me. I went to the bench, furious with myself. I had blown it! Coach Smith was not concerned with someone who could score points. I knew that. Everyone at this level could score. He wanted to see me do the little things: defense, box out, and rebound. I was so mad with myself that I took the towel the manager handed me and swung it to the ground in disgust — in the presence 10,000 onlookers in Carmichael Auditorium.

Coach Smith had witnessed this little fiasco. Very quickly and quietly, he walked down the bench and knelt in front of me. He simply said, "David, don't ever embarrass me, and I won't embarrass you." Then he walked back to his seat on the bench without saying another word.

I knew the one rule, and I had clearly broken it.

But I never did again. From that moment on, I disciplined myself to control my responses and never embarrass him or the team again. I knew I had to be governed from the inside out.

Develop Trust

Teaching personal responsibility and self-discipline through this inside-out approach requires the kind of meaningful and respectful relationship between leader and followers that will develop trust. We all respected Coach Smith. We truly did not want to embarrass him. The crucial dimension in all communication is the relationship. When the relationship is right, we can almost communicate without words. Coach Smith could give us a look in practice that sometimes communicated more than words.

And the key to all relationships is time. Someone once said that the way kids spell love is T-I-M-E.

Employees need time too. A leader should examine whether he is spending quality and quantity time with work associates in order to develop trust.

Is your door always open? Ged Doughton, a former player in the 1970s and now a successful Charlotte businessman, remembers being in Coach Smith's office one time when the intercom buzzed. The secretary announced, "Senator So-and-So is on the phone for you." Coach Smith said, "Tell him I'm with a player and I'll call him back." Ged felt as important as the president of the United States, and Coach Smith's action fostered a deep sense of trust and loyalty.

How then should you spend time developing trust? It is best accomplished with the private visit in your office or the work associate's office, the relaxed lunch, the private chat over coffee — in other words, a time when you are focused solely and specifically on that person, his fears, concerns, needs, hopes, and interests.

Do you as a leader spend time like this with your employees? Do they think you intimately care about their lives? Would employees feel they could come to you and share their concerns, or do they see you locked in your corner office with the view, unreachable and unapproachable?

The second way Coach Smith helped develop relational trust was by refusing to let us compare ourselves with one another. He constantly urged us to know our limitations as well as our strengths. He felt each individual was an important cog in the entire machinery. If he felt any envy among us, he would immediately confront us and remind us of the uniqueness of our own personal giftedness. Over and over again he would say, "Improve your strengths and weaknesses, and the team will become better."

At the beginning of every season, he developed team goals. At the end of the season, every individual would have personal goals for becoming a better player. Coach Smith was always brutally honest during this interview. If he did not think you would play, even with hard work, he would tell you. If he thought transferring was your best option in order to play, he would help you find the right school. But your name would still be on his letterman's list, and he would always consider you a part of the Carolina family.

In this way, Coach Smith taught us that as the individual improves, it allows the whole team to improve.

Nelson Mandela stated this principle eloquently. He said, "We ask ourselves, 'Who am I to be brilliant, gorgeous, talented, and fabulous?' Actually, who are you not to be? You are a child of God. Your playing small doesn't serve the world. There's nothing enlightened about shrinking so that other people won't feel insecure around you. We were born to manifest the glory of God within us…And as we let our own light shine, we unconsciously give other people permission to do the same. As we are liberated from our own fear, our presence automatically liberates others."

Mandela was simply stating the obvious: when the individual unleashes the enormous, unique potential he has, the team becomes better. He was also confronting the damage that occurs when a person starts comparing himself with someone else. It can only be destructive.

Coach Smith was brilliant when he refused to let us compare ourselves with one another. He knew this kind of comparison was deadly to a team. It destroyed the uniqueness of the individual and could abort the need for claiming personal responsibility. The snare of comparison keeps our inexhaustible godly qualities locked inside us.

Work Hard in the Off-season

Coach Smith also taught us to work hard in the off-season in order to become the best individual players we could. He placed that kind of motivation within us. We took responsibility for our lives. And we were willing to pay to price in self-discipline to make the team better.

William Oncken, president of the Oncken Corporation in Dallas, Texas, said, "Successful coaches bring many skills to the table. They provide their people the opportunity to become the best they can possibly be. The coaches set up an environment wherein people feel good about themselves, believe in themselves, care about each other, and feel empowered to make a meaningful contribution." That's another way of saying, "As the individual improves, so does the team."

In our annual performance evaluations in the church I serve, I ask each staff person what conferences they plan to attend the next year or what courses they are going to take for professional development. We're willing to pay for it. We know that as they become better leaders, the organization is greatly enhanced.

Moreover, we borrowed something from the world of academia. After the first seven years, each staff leader takes a two-month sabbatical. They have to submit to the Personnel Committee a description of where they are going, what they plan to do, and what they are trying to learn. We then try to pay for most of it.

These two simple requirements, annual leadership development and a sabbatical after seven years of faithful service (repeated after five more years on the staff), are our version of working hard during the off-season. And they have done wonders to develop personal responsibility.

Collins and Porras in *Built to Last* state that the extraordinary success of visionary companies is not so much because of superior intellect or supposed success secrets, but most often because the workers in the companies demand so much of themselves. "Becoming and remaining a visionary company requires oodles of plain old-fashioned discipline, hard work and a visceral revulsion to any tendency toward smug self-satisfaction."

Coach Smith's teams became better and better largely because individual players took personal responsibility and became better players.

It's a simple secret to success for all corporations and teams.

Thought for the Day

If you want to make the team better, become better yourself.

Game Plan

- Teach personal responsibility
- Teach self-discipline
- Use an inside-out approach
- Develop trust
- Work hard in the off-season

Team Practice

- To what extent do you take personal responsibility for what happens to you?
- How do you demonstrate personal responsibility?
- How do you reinforce personal responsibility in others?
- What can your organization do to build a sense of trust?

7

THE POWER OF POSITIVE WORDS

"By how many points do you think we'll win?"

A few years ago, Carolina was playing Duke in Durham. It has always been a very difficult place to play because of the incredibly vocal fans. I played in Cameron Indoor Stadium 25 years ago, and we called them the Cameron Crazies then, too.

Before this particular game, the Tar Heels were huddled in the locker room. The "crazies" were yelling, jumping, and screaming. The band was blaring the Duke fight song. Even in the locker room, the noise was almost deafening.

As the time came to run onto the floor, everyone knew they would be resoundingly booed. The Carolina players mentally readied themselves for every possible indignity.

Coach Smith calmly walked into the huddle and looked his players in the eye. He said two things: "First," he said, "Isn't it amazing at this moment that a billion people in China don't care one bit who wins this game." Then he paused. Then he continued, "Isn't it going to be fun to shut them up?!?"

Carolina won the game.

In explaining how Coach Smith motivated his teams, I would be remiss if I did not talk about his extraordinary ability to be a positive encourager in tough game situations. Carolina comebacks and victories under Coach Smith are now legendary. However, few people know what really went on in the huddles when strategic decisions were made that led to those victories. Often it was Coach Smith's ability to encourage through positive words that inspired incredible performances.

In one particular game, Carolina was down by several points with a little more than a minute to go. During a time-out everyone came to the bench with concerned looks on their faces. Coach Smith just smiled.

He turned to Ademola Okulaja and asked, "By how many points do you think we'll win?" Okulaja responded, "I think we'll win by five."

Then Coach Smith asked the same question of Antawn Jamison, who answered, "I think we'll win by three."

They won by five.

No one completely understands the power of encouraging words on another person. We know discouraging words spread negativism and a defeatist attitude among sports teams, families, and companies like a spark to wood after a 60-day drought.

One of my favorite illustrations is about a man who wanted revenge against someone who had severely hurt him, so he went to the devil to buy an instrument of pain he could use against his enemy. He looked at one weapon and asked what it was.

The devil said, "That's slander, and it's very effective. It's worth a million dollars."

The man then pointed to another instrument and asked what it was.

"That is a furious temper," the devil said. "I use it often to break apart relationships and hurt people. It is also worth a million dollars."

The man finally pointed to one instrument on the far end of the table. "What is that and how much will it cost?"

"Oh, no," replied the devil. "That's not for sale. It's called discouragement, and it is my most valuable weapon."

Discouragement is a powerful negative force. "Sticks and stones may break my bones, but words will never hurt me." Ever heard that one? It's a lie. Words do hurt. They divide and discourage us as nothing else.

Yet, on the other hand, how powerful positive words can be! They can inspire like nothing else.

This principle even works in the animal kingdom. Geese, for example, can fly 72 percent farther in formation than alone. Do you know why they honk as they fly? Because the goose at the point of the V cannot turn his neck to see if the other geese are still following him. The force of the headwind blowing against him is so furious that if he turned his neck, it would instantly snap in two. So the other geese honk to tell the leader not to quit, to let him know they are still in formation behind him, still supporting him. They honk their encouragement.

Become a Positive Encourager

You cannot give out encouraging words, however, if positive thoughts don't fill your own heart. It is my belief that Coach Smith thought positively, therefore he easily became a positive encourager.

In 1968 George Karl was a very highly recruited point guard from Penn Hills, Pennsylvania. He had narrowed his choices to Duke or Maryland. Coach Smith entered the recruiting scene late with George, but decided he really wanted him.

George was not very encouraging when Coach Smith visited.

"What are our chances?" Coach Smith asked Karl.

"About one in ten," he answered.

"I like those odds," Smith said. He convinced Karl to visit Carolina. George loved the campus, the program, the players, and, especially, Coach Smith. He signed a scholarship with UNC soon after his visit.

A leader can't give positive, encouraging words if he's not a positive, encouraging person himself. It all starts here!

How important are positive words? They can mean the difference between quitting and staying in the game long enough to win.

In his early years in baseball, Jackie Robinson, the first black player in the major leagues, was ready to quit. He could not stomach the continual racist slurs thrown at him. One day, when he was particularly ready to give it up, he brazenly decided to steal home in a very important game. Like a wild man, he rushed from third, sliding under the catcher's tag. As he ran to the dugout, a little boy right behind the dugout kept yelling at him, "Way to go, Jackie! Way to go! Keep it up!"

The boy's words kept ringing in his ears. "Keep it up!" And at that moment, Jackie Robinson decided not to quit.

Amazing, isn't it? Several simple sentences from an unknown little boy allowed baseball and the entire sports world to keep one of its greatest players. A few positive words of encouragement outweighed all the discouraging words of the critics.

One time during my ministry I wanted to give up, too. Life's pressures had become too great for me to bear, and I wanted to quit. I remember one night when my wife, Marilynn, and I were on vacation. I was sitting on the edge of the bed at two in the morning, staring out the window at the water.

Marilynn awakened and noted my odd behavior. "What's wrong?" she asked.

"I want to quit," I said. "Ministry is too difficult."

She leaned over to me, took my hand, and quietly said, "I believe in you, David."

That's all I needed to hear. I persevered.

The tough time did pass. Ministry became meaningful to me again. The church started to surge forward. How glad I am now that I didn't quit. How glad I am that someone spoke encouraging words to me.

Coach Smith placed such an emphasis on positive words that he never allowed one player to criticize another player. In fact, he even became angry with me once for criticizing a *football* player.

During my freshman year, Carolina had just lost a tough football game. The team had two talented quarterbacks. One was a gifted option quarterback and fine runner. The other was a fine passer who later played in the NFL. For this game, the coach had decided to play the option quarterback, relegating the passer to the bench.

It just so happened that the passing quarterback was a high school friend of my older brother, Howard. In the locker room after a practice that followed the football game, I mentioned to a teammate that I questioned the football coach's wisdom in not playing the passer, proudly pointing out that he was my brother's friend.

Coach Smith overheard my comments. He approached me with fire flashing from his eyes. He told me in no uncertain terms that I had no right to question the football coach's judgment, reminding me that we were not only a basketball family, but also a university family. "Don't ever do that again publicly," he told me as he walked away.

I was embarrassed, but I knew Coach Smith was right. To this day I watch my words when I say something publicly about another person. I understand that my silence carefully guards his reputation. It also helps guarantee unity.

There's an old maxim that says, "If you can't say something good, don't say anything at all."

That's dead wrong. Say something good! Say a lot of good, encouraging words to people. They can make a tremendous difference in their lives. Positive words can change a life. They can spark a team to victory.

See Victory in Your Mind

One of Carolina's most famous comeback victories occurred against Duke in 1973. The Tar Heels came from eight down with 17 seconds to go to tie the game at the buzzer, go into overtime, and eventually win. A key player in this victory was Bobby Jones. He told me that when Coach Smith called timeout with 17 seconds on the clock, the team came to the bench fairly dejected.

With a calm voice and a wry smile, Coach said, "Let's have some fun here. Let's decide we're going to win this game."

"Then he turned to me," Jones remembered, "and said, 'Bobby, you're going to make these two free throws. Then we're going to put on the trap and we're going to steal the ball. And if we don't get the steal, we'll foul them immediately. Then we'll talk some more at the next timeout."

"So I made the free throws and we put the trap on. Someone deflected the ball and we got possession. We scored a lay-up and immediately fouled again. We called timeout and went to the huddle. The crowd was tense and loud. Coach just sat down, all calm and relaxed, even smiling.

'Okay, here's what we need to do,' he said. 'They'll miss the free throws and we'll go down and score. Then call timeout again.'"

That's exactly what happened. "We're now down by two with a few seconds left," Jones continued. "In the huddle, he told us to throw a half-court pass to Walter Davis, for Walter to take no more than two dribbles, shoot the ball, score — and we would win in overtime.

"It was amazing. It all happened exactly as he said. And when we went into overtime, no one was really celebrating. We just knew that if we did what he said, we'd win. It was as if he had scripted it. But what was so amazing was how calm and positive he was in the huddle. And because he was so positive and encouraging, so were we!"

Coach Smith could see the victory in his mind, and that's what he transmitted to the players. Over and over he stimulated them to win by planting in their minds an image of how a big win could be achieved. Then he reinforced that image with positive words. As Jones said, it was almost as if he scripted the victory. It was that clear to him.

On the first day of practice one year, Coach Smith had each player climb a ladder and cut down a part of the net. This team was not predicted to do very well, so he wanted to plant in their minds from day one what it would feel like to cut down a net after winning a championship.

After that first practice, they went into the locker room and had a huge celebration. They draped the newly cut nets over the 1993 championship trophy and took a team picture around it. Later each player put a copy of that picture in his locker, to help visualize the championship.

Another season, the team members opened their lockers after the first practice and found a picture of the basketball arena in Charlotte. They knew it had been designated as the location for the Final Four that year. The scoreboard in the picture showed the Tar Heels winning the national championship. Coach Smith wanted them to see the victory in their minds.

Believe in Others

Roy Williams, one of Coach Smith's former assistants and presently head coach at Kansas University, shared a similar experience from the national championship game against Georgetown in 1982.

"David," he told me, "it was the greatest single experience I've ever had in my life about how positive encouragement can change people's attitudes in a tense situation. We were down by one and when the guys came to the timeout with about forty seconds to play, I really thought we might lose the game. I had believed we were the best team and were destined to win. But at that moment, I began to doubt."

Roy carefully studied the looks on the players' faces, and he believed they also thought they were going to lose the game.

"We coaches were kneeling down in front of the players," Williams continued, "and we knew the coaches were going to determine the outcome of this game. Coach Smith then proceeded to tell the players what we were going to do. He said to penetrate and look for the best shot possible. But what was probably going to happen, he said, would be a penetration that would allow us to kick it to the backside. We'd then get a shot and knock it in. He said not to worry if we missed the shot, because we would have the other side covered with rebounding. And if we missed and they got the rebound, not to worry because we'd foul them and they'd miss the free throw under that kind of pressure.

"I can't explain it. Suddenly their spirits lifted. I checked the scoreboard again to see if somehow we'd gotten ahead in the game. And then, as the players left the huddle, he patted Michael Jordan on the back and said, 'Knock it in, Michael.' He knew the shot was going to come to him.

"Needless to say, the rest is history," Williams concluded. "It happened exactly as he designed it."

Many fans have heard this story. However, what they may not know is what Coach Smith said to Matt Doherty in that same huddle. Doherty added the following account.

"Right before that timeout, I had missed a crucial shot, one that could have put us up by three with 1:19 to go. Instead, they went down and Sleepy Floyd scored to put Georgetown up by one. That's when we called timeout. When I went to that huddle, I felt awful. I had let all my teammates and coaches down. Coach Smith outlined the next play, like everyone has heard.

"As we broke from the huddle," Doherty continued, "he told Michael to knock it down. But what people don't know is that as I left the huddle, he said the same thing to me. Can you imagine? He was anticipating that

I was feeling down from missing the previous shot. He wanted me to be confident in case I was forced to take the final shot. His constant encouragement gave all of us confidence."

Coach Smith believed in his players, and he encouraged them to believe in themselves, even when the odds were against them.

Matt Doherty also shared an interesting way Coach Smith developed confidence through encouragement in practice. "He knew I was a smart player who competed, and I could pass the ball and do little things like that," Doherty said. "And I knew that if I did the little things I would play.

"So I really began to work on my screens. I wanted to be the best screener on the team. I remember him pulling me aside one day and saying I was the best screener in the country. It made me feel so good, I started working even harder on my screens. At clinics during the summer I told the kids that Coach Smith said I was the best screener in the country. I'd go downtown and meet a pretty girl, and I'd tell her that Coach Smith said I was the best screener in the country. It filled my black book with phone numbers! Anyway, his encouragement motivated me to do the little things better than ever."

Sometimes, of course, it is necessary to show disapproval. But Coach Smith always managed to do it in a positive way.

Lee Dedmon, a 1967–71 letterman and co-most valuable player of the 1971 ACC Tournament, said, "Oh, he can get angry. But he gets angry at the action, not the person. He often expresses his anger to groups, not individuals. He won't hesitate to bounce some chalk off your head if you're going to sleep while watching game film."

Mitch Kupchak said, "He can throw chairs with his eyes. I always felt that when he simply said, 'Change jerseys,' and moved someone in practice from the first to the second team. You knew his disapproval. But it was always done in such a way that you never felt belittled. In fact, you always felt it was best for the team, and somehow for you too!"

Ronald Reagan received his highest ratings ever right after he was shot in 1981. One year later, he received his lowest ratings ever, a 32 percent approval rating. His underlings were terribly discouraged. Sensing this, he gathered them all together and said, "Don't worry. Every thing will be fine. I'll just go out and get shot again!" His ability to put a positive slant on a discouraging situation helped his staff get through a difficult time.

A great leader has the ability to impart to his followers a positive attitude that can overcome anything. Ken Blanchard, author of the enormously successful book, *The One Minute Manager*, said, "Of all the concepts that I have taught over the years, the most important is about 'catching people doing things right.' There is little doubt in my mind that the key to developing people is to catch them doing something right and praising their performance. The minute you begin talking about catching someone doing things right, praising that person, and letting him or her know you noticed their good performance, that person's attention perks up."

No leader should ever underestimate the power of positive words. When you're managing by walking around, a hand on the shoulder and a statement like "I really appreciate how much you mean to this corporation" go a long way. Everyone likes to be praised. Look in the eyes of your child when you offer praise. Remember, an adult is often just a grown-up child. We need encouragement just as much as they do.

A good question for all leaders to ask themselves would be, "Do the people who work with and under me feel positive encouragement coming from me, no matter what the odds?" People feel cheated if all they ever receive from a leader is information. All workers in every organization need information, but they need even more huge doses of inspiration and congratulation. They need positive encouragement.

Walter Bennis, in a speech delivered on C-Span entitled "Managing People Is Like Herding Cars," said, "All leaders expect positive outcomes The glass is not half-empty or half-full, but always full." That expresses the necessity of a positive outlook.

Preparation Fosters a Positive Outlook

While positive encouragement is a necessary principle for any successful leader, an important part of Coach Smith's ability to be positive, to believe when everything seemed impossible, was his absolutely thorough preparation.

Every day Coach Smith would post a thought for the day on the practice schedule. Each player had to read it and recite it if called on during the practice. If he couldn't do it, the individual and/or the team would have to run.

One of Coach Smith's favorite thoughts for the day was, "Luck is when preparation meets opportunity." John Lotz told me that in the 35 plus years he has known Coach Smith, he has never heard him say, "Good luck." Not once. "He simply doesn't believe in luck," Lotz said. "You win by being prepared, not by being lucky."

It's fascinating to study how Coach Smith prepared for an opponent in light of his commitment to the team above the individual. First, he insisted that his teams be the best-conditioned in America. He vowed that we would never lose because our opposition was in better shape than we were.

Moreover, we prepared for every situation. In our two-hour practices, each one timed to the minute, we spent time going over every possible game situation. What would we do if there's a minute left and we're down by two? Ahead by two? There are 10 seconds left, we're down by one, and we have the ball? We were prepared for those situations before the game ever started.

"During the 1983 season," Buzz Peterson told me, "we were playing Tulane. We were in triple overtime. Down by three. Coach Smith drew up a play on his paper. He said, 'Buzz, you're here. Matt, you're here. Michael, you're here.' I remember thinking there sure were a lot of lines going all over the place, but I remembered where I was supposed to go. Something in practice reminded me.

"I came out of the huddle and looked at Matt and asked, 'Do you know what you're supposed to do?' He said, 'Yeah.' Then he asked me, 'Do you know what you're supposed to do?' And I said, 'Yeah.' Then he said, 'Well, let's do what we're supposed to do!'

"The only thing I remembered was to go to a certain area. I saw the ball go over my head, then Michael had it in his hands and was shooting a three. We went into another overtime and won the game. We were a better team, but we didn't play that well. But we won, I think, because we were really prepared and in better shape!"

Coach Smith was so thorough in his simulation of game situations that he once had the team practice the same drill for almost four straight months. Every day in practice he set up the same situation: Pearce Landry guarded Jerry Stackhouse with 10 seconds left on the clock, down by one, and the opposing team had possession of the ball. Landry's assignment: prevent Stackhouse from catching the ball for five seconds, and force a violation and a turnover.

Understandably, Landry wearied of repeating this simulation, often wondering why he had to do this hackneyed drill over and over again.

Then Carolina played Wake Forest in Winston-Salem. For most of the game UNC was down by 15 points — which is where the Tar Heels were at the 12:00 minute timeout in the second half. Smith called the team over and said, "At the 8:00 minute timeout, we'll be down by ten. Then at 4:00 we'll be down by five. Then it's anyone's game."

That is exactly what happened. They kept whittling the lead down until, with 10 seconds left, UNC was down by one and Wake Forest had the ball. Smith called a timeout and summoned Pearce Landry to enter the game. "Pearce, it's your job to keep Randolph Childress (Wake's superstar guard)from catching the ball."

The ball was handed to the Wake player inbounding the pass. Carolina applied pressure. Wake tried to get the ball to Childress, their best free-throw shooter. But after guarding Stackhouse in exactly the same situation every day for four months, guarding Childress was a piece of cake for Landry. Childress never touched the ball.

The five second call came and the ball was awarded to Carolina. Donald Williams got the ball, drove the right side of the lane, and hit a running one-hander as time expired to win the game.

When your preparation is that precise, you can see the victory in your mind and you can achieve it on the court.

Woody Durham, the Tar Heels' radio announcer, shared another story regarding Coach Smith's legendary preparation. "I have always believed that his preparation is the key to his success. I will never forget 1990. Carolina was not considered to be one of the stronger teams going into the NCAA tournament. It may have been the lowest seed Carolina had ever had. They were the eighth seed and got shipped out to the Midwest regional in Austin, Texas. We won the first-round game and then had to be matched up against the number-one team in the nation in Oklahoma.

"At that time we were doing Coach Smith's pre-game interview during the pre-game meal. While the team and the assistant coaches were down in the dining room, I would go to his hotel suite to do the pre-game interview. I remember knocking on the door of his hotel room. He came to the door and let me in. He was still watching some Oklahoma tape. It was Oklahoma versus Kansas. He knew Kansas did a lot of things like us, and he was looking for any advantage. I watched him run the tapes back and forth, over and over again. He studied them intently. Finally, he sat back in the chair and said, 'I think I know them pretty well. Now, if I can just translate it to the players.'

"About six hours later, Rick Fox made a lay-up in the last second. Carolina upset the number-one team in the country and moved ahead in the tournament. I'm convinced he knew Oklahoma's tendency to over-play on defense and he was prepared to run that play, in that situation, if necessary, before the game ever began."

Durham told another story that illustrates the same principle. "It was North Carolina versus Virginia in the late 1980s. Virginia had the ball with a few seconds left. If they make the shot, they win. During the time-out huddle, Coach Smith reached for the clipboard to diagram something. He diagrammed the play Virginia was going to run. He turned to Scott Williams and told him they were going to inbound the ball to Richard Morgan. Morgan would then come left of the foul circle and take the jump shot from that point. He told Scott to release from his man when Morgan moved left from the jump circle. 'When you release,' he said, 'I want you to leap in the air, and I believe you can get a hand on his shot.' Then he smiled and said, 'And after you block the shot, just run into the locker room to the cheers of our fans.'

"So Virginia threw the ball to Richard Morgan. He dribbled to the left of the circle and went up in the air; Scott Williams ran toward him, tipped the ball with two fingers, and then ran into the dressing room. Carolina won the game. It happened just as Coach Smith diagrammed it. You should have seen Scott Williams's face as he described this to me. He wondered if Coach Smith was some kind of soothsayer or psychic!

"But he's simply very well prepared. Coach had looked at so many tapes of Virginia that he had spotted a pattern for a last-second play. He had seen them run this same play in two games, so he believed they would do it again. There was no luck involved. He was simply prepared."

Vision Fosters Preparation

I believe Coach Smith's best preparation, however, did not consist of simulating game situations or studying the opposition but in tenaciously believing in his philosophy. Yes, he was ready for Virginia's final play. But the defensive commitment to have his big men expose themselves on a pick is what allowed Scott Williams to switch and block the shot.

Day in and day out we spent more time in practice going over his offensive and defensive schemes than we did memorizing the plays of our opponents. We did become familiar with them. However, we spent most of our practice time going over our philosophy. We repeatedly ran through our preparation until we were ready to play. Coach Smith concentrated on teamwork rather than on the opposition. He felt that this would win games — and 80 percent of the time he was right.

What a leadership insight! Too many leaders spend most of their time studying their opposition instead of perfecting their own teams. That's not to say we should never study others. We can glean some important insights from analyzing competitors. However, our greatest productivity comes in performing our vision well. If that vision does not consistently win, perhaps the vision is inadequate. A good vision motivating a high-performing team that places the team above the individual should win in spite of what the opposition is doing.

Practice prepared our team to face the opposition. Coach Smith stayed centered on what was most important for us to perform. I believe this preparation allowed him to focus on the things that were important, not urgent.

When talking about urgent tasks that leaders too often respond to but then later regret, Charles Hummel said, "The appeal of these tasks seems irresistible, and they devour our energy. But in perspective, their deceptive prominence fades; and with a sense of loss, we recall the vital tasks we pushed aside. We realize that we have become slaves to the tyranny of the urgent."

The city of Charlotte recently commissioned a study regarding how the city can continually be on the cutting edge of growth in the twenty-first century. The study's emphasis was not on attracting industries from outside Charlotte to move here. Instead, the emphasis was on Charlotte's major, already-established, successful industries to continue to do what they do well. This, the study concluded, would better foster expanded growth plus naturally attract new industries thereafter. I think Coach Smith as a leader would enthusiastically endorse this conclusion.

Coach Smith concentrated on his vision and specifically how he thought a team should play together. He spent hours each day carefully teaching this vision. We were aware of the other team and what they did. But what drove us was our philosophy. We performed this vision at peak performance. And we won 80 percent of our games!

Positive words, plus positive envisioning, plus a positive vision equals success…to the tune of 879 successes for Coach Smith!

Thought for the Day

Positive words can change a life and spark a team.

Game Plan

- Be a positive encourager
- See victory in your mind
- Believe in others
- Preparation fosters a positive outlook
- Vision fosters preparation

Team Practice

- How do you encourage others?
- How do you demonstrate that you believe in others?
- How do you show disapproval in a positive way?
- What can your organization do to foster positive encouragement?

PASSING ON
WHAT YOU KNOW

"If they learned anything from me, I'm grateful."

On April 18, 1994, Coach Smith received the Apple Award for Distinguished Achievement from Kansas University. In presenting the award, given annually to a School of Education alumnus, Chancellor Gene A. Budig said, "Dean Smith is a world-class teacher. His players always reflect the skills and values he acquired as a student-athlete at the University of Kansas."

Every great leader is also a teacher and mentor. His concern is not simply for himself, but to teach what he has learned to those who share his passion. Coach Smith's basketball family tree has produced many coaches who have taken his vision of team before the individual to every level imaginable — from junior high leagues to the professional ranks.

I believe his passion in life is to teach young people how to play basketball and that he would be content coaching at a small Division III school. If he had no media attention, no ability for television cameras to reach him in a high school gym, he would easily adjust. I think he would like to announce that basketball try-outs will be on such and such a day, have kids come out who really love the game and simply want to play it for no other reason, and then start teaching. The only trouble is, he would be such a successful coach that within a year the press would be swarming all over him.

Coach Smith's passion for teaching started out as a passion for learning. "Whenever you talk about Dean Smith being a teacher of the game of basketball," Coach Bob Knight said, "you must first acknowledge that he was a student of the game of basketball. He spent countless hours talking the game of basketball with experts from his earliest years. And, in being a very good student, he put himself in a very good position to be an excellent teacher. He has taught basketball the way it is meant to be played. He gets the kids to work together unselfishly and to play in such a way that they receive recognition through team accomplishments. That's his underlying philosophy."

Michael Quigley, dean of the graduate school at St. Rivier College in Nashua, New Hampshire, wrote an article titled, "The Leader as Learner." In it he suggests that leaders must constantly be developing personal intellectual habits as well as the ability to analyze and interpret information for the purpose of strategic decision-making. In other words, the leader who is a teacher or mentor must also be a student. That's why Bob Knight suggested that being a great student of basketball was Coach Smith's greatest asset as a teacher.

This principle has been discovered by the corporate world as well as academia. For example, Richard C. Bartlett, vice chairman of Mary Kay Holding Corporation, says one of that corporation's key accomplishments has been to develop a culture of success that stresses continuous learning as a corporate "given." The leader who is teacher must first be a learner.

Coach Smith's learning and teaching genes run deep in his family. With both parents being schoolteachers, it was natural for him to become a teacher. Alfred Smith, his father, won the state basketball championship in 1934 at Emporia High School. He taught a dogged commitment to team play.

"I practically grew up in a gym," Coach Smith told me, "and I went to a couple of basketball clinics with my dad. When I was in college, though, Dr. Phog Allen wanted me to go into medicine. I guess I enrolled in one pre-med course, but my real interest was always in coaching."

His mother also made an impact upon Smith as an educator. In 1988 he gave $50,000 to Kansas University to establish the Vesta Marie Edwards Smith Scholarship in Education. It's named in honor of Smith's mother and is given to students in the elementary education program. The scholarship is awarded on the basis of monetary need and academic promise to kids from Allen, Lyon, and Shaver counties in Kansas — places where Coach Smith's mother taught for 40 years.

Coach Smith was on the 1952 national championship team at Kansas University. After this successful season, Phog Allen wrote all the members of the team:

> It's been great fun. But twenty-five to thirty years from now you boys will radiate and multiply your recollections of your struggles and successes and your defeats. All these will be rolled into a fine philosophy of life, which will give you durable satisfactions down through the years. It has been wonderful for me to be so closely associated with such a fine group of outstanding Kansas men as you.
>
> Sincerely,
> Dr. Forrest C. Allen, 'Doc'

So, Coach Smith was a student of the game from his father and Phog Allen. In a way, they both mentored him. He learned the vision of the team before the individual from both of them. Basketball was a vehicle to teach his vision of team over the individual but also to teach young men a philosophy of life. Now coaches who played under him and shared coaching responsibilities with him are doing the same.

How did Coach Smith not only teach his players, but particularly his players and assistants who have now become coaches? How intentional was he? Was there a program or philosophy that guided him as a teacher and mentor?

Intentional and Imitational Mentoring

I interviewed a number of men who coached with Dean Smith about how he mentored them. Was there a program he set up to teach them? Did he intentionally mentor them as future coaches? From the different answers, I discovered two different approaches to mentoring, both of which Coach Smith modeled.

The first approach is intentional mentoring. Many of those presently in the basketball coaching profession — Larry Brown, Phil Ford, George Karl, John Kuester, Eddie Fogler, Buzz Peterson, and King Rice, for example — were all point guards for Coach Smith's teams. During the preseason and the regular season, these basketball "quarterbacks" regularly met with Coach Smith about his overall basketball philosophy and his game-by-game personal strategy. These sessions were intentional mentoring classes that laid the foundation for the next generation of coaches. Even after they became head coaches, these men would meet with Coach Smith for several days each summer, in a kind of continuing education program.

While these were intentional sessions on the principles of coaching, most of Coach Smith's mentoring flowed out of his peripatetic teaching style. The word *peripatetic* means to walk up and down and refers to the kind of teaching that takes place while moving or traveling from one location to another.

This is the style Jesus used in teaching his disciples how to do ministry after his departure. He first built a close, meaningful relationship with them. They spent three years with him, observing what he did and how he did it. As he went about doing his ministry, he simply told his disciples to pay attention, to ask questions if they didn't understand anything, and then he told them to go and do likewise.

Similarly, Coach Smith had students who loved basketball work with him. He found teachable moments during the everyday routine of practice and training. He permitted interaction. He allowed questions and asked for input. As the students drew closer and closer to him, they never stopped observing and asking questions. Later, they adapted what they had learned to their own head coaching experiences.

For example, Eddie Fogler, head of the University of South Carolina's basketball program, told me that Coach Smith never actually taught him to coach. "I simply had the experience and the exposure of working with him," he said. "I was in all those meetings and closed practices. I saw how he handled the players' meetings. I saw how he organized the travel plans. I saw first hand the ups and downs. There was no formula he took us through. Now I draw from those experiences and try to apply them as best as I can here at South Carolina."

One time Coach Fogler was on the bench next to Coach Smith in a tight game. Coach Smith turned to him and asked what he thought they should do in this situation. "I thought for a few moments, then gave him my opinion," Fogler recalled. "He didn't do what I suggested, but he did turn to me and say, 'I just wanted to see if you were paying attention.'"

George Karl, coach of the NBA's Milwaukee Bucks, told me that it's a privilege to be with Coach Smith every summer for four or five days. "We talk a lot about basketball and a lot about life," Karl said. "He's never tried to impose his system on me. He's simply been available, and I do a lot of observing and asking questions. I guess that's how he mentored me as a coach."

The on-the-job training he learned from Coach Smith is what sticks in assistant coach Phil Ford's mind. "I learned largely how to do things by observing his philosophy. The hardest thing is to get that philosophy out of his head and into my heart, and that's the objective of coaching. But I learned how to do that by observing him and asking questions."

Coach Smith's intentional mentoring did not extend solely to his key players. For example, Roy Williams, Kansas University's very successful coach, never played on the varsity team at Carolina. "I had to start working for a living in college. So I worked in the intramural office and refereed basketball games, umpired softball games, or whatever needed to be done. I usually started at four in the afternoon, and I would go by and watch a little bit of practice beforehand. Practices were closed, but Coach Smith let me stay. He sensed I really wanted to coach. I still have those notes from the freshman and varsity practices I observed.

"When I was in graduate school, they asked me to work the summer camp because I was a good official. I refereed the scrimmages at night. After college I got a high school job and stayed there five years. But I continued to work the summer camps, and eventually Coach Smith asked me to be an assistant. But, you know, he has never had a set agenda for mentoring me. I simply observed, asked a lot of questions, saw how he did it, then adapted his style into my own. I think that every day I was with him he was preparing me to have my own program."

Bill Guthridge, Coach Smith's successor at Carolina, said he thought that Coach Smith "wanted all of us to become head coaches, or at least to have the opportunity. He encouraged us, both on and off the court, always to think like we were head coaches. He would constantly ask us, 'What would you do here if you were the head coach? Give me some suggestions.' Then he would digest our input. Sometimes he would use what we'd suggest, sometimes not. But we felt included. And I think this helped prepare us for that day when we would be head coaches ourselves. Of course, it's always easier to give suggestions than to live with decisions, but I think I was as prepared as I could have been to follow him."

In talking with many of those who have become coaches after sitting under Coach Smith's tutelage, it is obvious that he had no formula for mentoring them. The similar thread woven through all their testimonies is the "teaching on the go" experience that he offered those who wanted to learn.

Stephen Covey described this type of teaching as "modeling and mentoring." He said, "You can only become a mentor to someone if you are first a model, an example, and then build a relationship. Many people, including entertainers and athletes, are models, but they have no meaningful relationship with their fans. If you are a model and have a relationship, you can be a true mentor ... and in a mature mentoring relationship, when you make mistakes, you do not destroy the faith of students because their faith is not based on you — it is based on the same set of principles."

The most significant learning occurs within the context of a relationship. Coach Smith gathered gifted people around him and allowed their friendship to grow. Then he allowed them to observe his genius, often asking for their input. He gave them every opportunity to learn from him as he performed his daily coaching responsibilities. They could ask any questions they wanted. Any question was a good question, he told them, if they didn't know the answer. Then, when the time came for them to become head coaches, they went and adapted his style to their own unique personality and setting. Their success speaks for itself.

To a larger group — all of his players, not just those who wanted to become coaches — Dean Smith engaged in what I call imitational mentoring. This is what some people would simply say is being an exemplar, or role model. For his other lettermen, and for many associates, his involvement with us as a friend was a model for how life should be lived and how leaders should lead. Many people joke with me and say I lead the church I serve like Coach Smith did the Carolina basketball program, I haven't spent much time with him personally since I graduated. However, I have constantly observed his leadership. I learned by observing then imitating. It wasn't intentional mentoring to train us as coaches, but imitational mentoring to teach us how to live and lead others.

Yet both approaches involve mentoring, influencing through leadership and example to be the best players and people possible.

This imitational mentoring is so effective that no one will ever know just how many people Coach Smith has affected. He is admired by many and copied by multitudes because of who he is. Indeed, because of his imitational mentoring in my own life, I'm now writing this book — which hopefully will extend the influence of Coach Smith to even more people.

Mentoring Future Generations

Therefore, Coach Smith's mentoring of his players, both intentionally and through imitation, will affect many generations to come.

For example, Bobby Jones is now the head basketball coach of Charlotte Christian High School. One of his former players is Luke Boythe, now a forward for the University of North Carolina at Greensboro. Here is how Boythe described what Jones has meant to him as a person first, and then as a player. "Coach Jones was genuinely concerned for us as individuals more than as athletes," he said. Boythe recalled Jones developing the team as young men, not just basketball players, and that he led by example.

It's no coincidence that the way Luke Boythe describes Bobby Jones is exactly the way former players talk about Coach Smith. That's what true mentoring is: taking your life and pouring it into another person, who then takes the same principles and pours them into another person, who then...You get the picture.

In fact, you almost get the picture that Luke Boythe is who he is because Coach Smith's father and Phog Allen were who they were in Coach Smith's life. Coach Smith passed that truth on to Jones, who gave it to Boythe, who, hopefully, in one way or another, will pass it on to the next generation.

All effective leaders lead with an eye to future generations. Max DePree, in his very popular book *Leadership Is an Art*, said, "Leaders are also responsible for future leadership. They need to identify, develop, and nurture future leaders." No one can lead exactly like you, but there are basic principles that are applicable for all generations. How I apply them for my generation may be different for those mentoring under me, but the principles themselves remain constant.

An outstanding example of how Coach Smith's mentoring has affected following generations of players and coaches can be found in the Chicago Bulls' six world championships. Now, I know Coach Smith never coached for Chicago. So let me explain what I mean.

The reason the Bulls have won six world championships is because of defense. That has been their imprimatur. "You don't know how lucky you are," Don Nelson, coach of the NBA's Dallas Mavericks, once told Bulls coach Phil Jackson, "when your two best offensive players are your two best defensive players." He was referring, of course, to Michael Jordan and Scottie Pippen. When Dennis Rodman, another great defensive player who loved to rebound, was added to the equation, the team was solidified.

Michael Jordan willed himself to become a great defensive player. But he also had a wonderful teacher and mentor, Dean Smith, who sensed Jordan's amazing athletic ability and saw his limitless professional career. Smith therefore pushed him early on to become a great defensive player. He constantly told Michael Jordan what he had told us: "Anyone can score on this level. Few really want to be great defensive players. But if you want to be a great player at the next level, you will have to play defense."

Jordan listened to his mentor. He became a great offensive and defensive player in college. This was most unusual for a young player. Most simply want to score and have little to do with the grinding, exhausting, in-the-trenches work of defense. But Jordan had learned from Smith that defense wins games, and winning was his highest priority. He ultimately hungered for championships, not MVP trophies. In fact, early in his career he mentioned to reporters how he yearned one day to be named the NBA's defensive player of the year as well as the league MVP.

Most people snickered that it couldn't be done. NBA pundits thought that it would require too much energy on both ends of the court for a player to accomplish such a feat. In fact, Jan Hubbard, then with the Dallas *Morning News*, said as much in one of his articles. Evidently Jordan read it, for when he did win both awards in the 1987–88 season, he reminded Hubbard of his mistake. That's how intensely competitive Michael Jordan is.

Then Scottie Pippen joined the NBA and the Chicago Bulls with tremendous raw skills and natural talent. He possessed quickness, jumping ability, and extraordinarily long arms — with an even wider span than Jordan's. It became evident early on that Pippen would offer the unique ability to guard every one on the floor, from a point guard to the center. He could cause major disruptions to another team if his defensive skills could be honed.

Enter Michael Jordan. Nothing in those early years helped Pippen more than playing against Michael Jordan every day in practice. Jordan made a commitment to teach Pippen how to play defense. He killed him every day in practice. Michael had a reputation for making or breaking his teammates, and Scottie offered a special project with potentially exceptional rewards. In essence, Jordan became Pippen's mentor.

Pippen responded in kind. Where other players might have been driven from the league because of Jordan's relentless pressure in practice, the young, gifted, voracious Pippen fought him at every corner. Michael Jordan knew this simple reality: if Pippen could guard Jordan every day in practice, he could guard anyone in the league. And he did. What's more, the Jordan–Pippen combination on the court became Chicago's lethal weapon. So powerful did the two become together that Jordan once said it was like having his twin on the court with him.

No one can predict what impact mentoring one gifted person can have on the future. Why has Chicago won six national championships? It is at least partly attributable to Dean Smith. When he taught Michael Jordan to play defense, he was teaching Scottie Pippen and all the other Bulls on those championship teams how to play defense. The results rest in the annals of NBA folklore and history.

Coach Smith believed the team to be more important than the individual. He doggedly taught that defense wins games. He believed he was preparing people for life, not just to be better basketball players. Those who played for him or coached with him observed him and learned these principles. They are now practicing the same things. And those working under Coach Smith's former assistants will one day pass these same truths on to the teams they coach.

No one could ultimately guess the numbers of people worldwide who, over the next decades, will be positively affected by Coach Smith because he mentored a few. That, in essence, is what teaching and mentoring is all about. An effective leader understands this truth and passes it on to those who work with him, those who will be leading long after he retires.

The leader who influences others to lead others is a leader without limitation. The more people you develop, the longer your legacy.

Leading Generation X

As I told different people about working on this project, many of them wanted me to ask Coach Smith for advice on how to lead Generation X. It appears members of this generation are different from previous generations and may need an altered leadership style.

I not only asked Coach Smith, I asked many other successful coaches how they dealt with Generation X. Their answers, which follow, were helpful and insightful.

"On this subject," Bob Knight said, "I feel like I'm on an island with sharks swimming all around. Leadership was so much easier when you weren't trying to do it all by yourself. You simply don't have the assistance you had fifteen years ago. Somewhere along the way parents have let kids get away with a whole lot more than mine did.

"So I think leadership today is much more difficult. You don't have the authority support from their parents. I always felt that demands placed on kids to improve behavior and performance were essential for their development. Even the school system has lessened those demands. There is a struggle in our society for what is right and wrong, acceptable and unacceptable. Kids now have a harder time figuring that out.

"Therefore, with this generation, I still keep the demands high. Maybe I'm even tougher today than I was fifteen years ago. Certainly a lot of people think so. But I'm trying to prepare kids for life, not a career in professional basketball. I can't let up. I keep pounding away, knowing I won't reach everyone. So my demands are the same for any team of any generation. That's the only way, in my opinion, you can coach this generation today. Demand the best from them. Discipline is still the key, although you will be lonelier and more isolated in this position than you have ever been before."

Phil Ford has a similar viewpoint. "You're talking about the difference between young men worrying about being drafted in the Vietnam War and guys today consumed with listening to LL Cool J. Yet I would say that you must deal with these guys the same way you dealt with previous generations. You make demands. You tell them what you want. Then you discipline them if they don't do it. You ultimately work with the kids who want to work. That's still the beginning point for success."

"You've got to recruit character," according to Kansas head coach Roy Williams. "Then you mold them into a team with clear expectations. You help them learn how to enjoy a teammate's success. But I simply won't recruit a kid from this generation who won't play team basketball or who has a bad attitude. I think that's the same for all generations."

I remember a particular player Roy Williams once recruited. He was a spectacular high school player, but during the recruiting season he publicly questioned "Roy's substitution pattern." Can you imagine? To this day I still call Coach Smith "Coach." Even now I can't bring myself to call him by his first name because of my deep respect for him. After this teenager's diatribe, which clearly questioned whether he would receive enough playing time to adequately prepare his professional career, Williams abruptly announced he was no longer recruiting this individual. Williams's way of leading Generation

X? Recruit young men who understand the nuances of team basketball!

Jerry West said that working with Generation X "has been the most difficult and challenging part of being a general manager in the NBA. They need to know the rules, just like our generation, and the rules need to be uniformly enforced. I think they are willing to respond as long as they know the expectations."

"I think you have to clearly let them know that the inmates are not going to be allowed to run the asylum," Matt Doherty said. "You have to tell them from day one to be on time. If not, the bus will roll without them. Otherwise, they won't ever believe you again and you'll lose the respect of the other guys. They're different than fifteen years ago, but that's still the way you must lead them."

George Karl offered an interesting insight into the origin of some of the difficulties in leading Generation X. "Part of the problem with the Generation X athlete today in the NBA is caused by marketing the wrong stuff," he said. "For example, the Seattle Supersonics never play the Los Angeles Lakers. It was always Payton versus O'Neal. Very seldom do you hear people talk about team assists and fundamentals." Karl remembered how Coach Smith hated stat sheets. "He didn't like them in the locker room because they emphasized the individual over the team," he continued.

"Today, in the NBA, you not only have to communicate something to the player, but also to his agent, his parents, sometimes his wife. Now his personal problems are not only team problems, but also national news. To deal with this generation, you simply have to communicate. You must demand your principles in games and practice. You have to have a degree of discipline and commitment. And when the players see the team winning and that they are getting better every year, most buy in. Those who don't probably need to go."

There is a similar approach to the way all of these coaches are dealing with Generation X, and it's echoed by Coach Smith. The bottom line is that people may be different, but the basic principles remain the same.

"When I accepted the job at Carolina," Coach Smith said, "the school demanded we recruit good people who were serious students. That certainly helps the leader accomplish the vision of the team above the individual. To help insure they are good people, we would talk to their high school coaches. We asked their teammates what they thought of the players we were recruiting. We talked to their high school teachers. As coaches, all of us tend to inflate our players. I know I have done that with players and the NBA. But teachers are generally good people who are good judges.

"In recruiting, you don't always take the greatest player, but the one who is a good player and also a serious student with good work habits. If you do this, with any generation, and then let them know what you expect, I think you can get any generation to perform. It's more difficult today, so you have to be more intentional when you recruit or hire. But good people properly motivated with clear expectations and lines of authority can still perform — even Generation X."

In talking with these successful coaches about Generation X, a common theme ran through their comments. They all affirmed it is a more difficult generation to lead and manage. But they all also said that people are people, and what motivated previous generations still motivates today.

That makes sense to me, especially after studying the leadership techniques of Coach Smith and other successful leaders. It seems they all support a principle-centered leadership style. Their principles, not the players' whims and fancies, guide their coaching. Therefore, they treat all people from all generations the same, because *the principles* are the same. They are inviolable laws in the relational realm, as real as gravity is in the physical realm.

When practiced, these principles work for all leaders.

Thought for the Day

Mentoring requires a relationship, not a formula.

Game Plan

- Be an intentional mentor

- Find teachable moments

- Value questions and input

- Be an imitational mentor

- Build relationships

- Set an example

Team Practice

- What steps do you take to pass on what you know?

- How do you demonstrate to others that you value their input?

- To what extent do you look for positive qualities in others?

- Do you consistently live in a way that reflects your values?

A COMMITMENT
TO CHARACTER

*"Your reputation is what other
people think of you. Character is
what you think of yourself."*

Jim Smithwick, now a physician, played for Coach Smith from 1962 to 1966. He was a member of the team that experienced perhaps the most traumatic, potentially debilitating moment in Coach Smith's career.

Carolina had just lost a heartbreaker to Wake Forest. The trip back to Chapel Hill was somewhat somber, even depressing. When the team bus pulled up to the gym, an eerie sight greeted the players: a dummy of Coach Smith swinging from a tree. Some angry students had hung him in effigy.

The team sat in stunned silence. Everyone waited for Coach Smith's response. Smithwick, who was a sophomore on that team, gave this account: "He looked at the dummy, then turned to us. He was not angry. He just said, 'Your reputation is what other people think of you. Character is what you think of yourself.' Then Coach got off the bus and left."

"Billy Cunningham ran off the bus and angrily tore down the dummy. But I'll never forget Coach Smith's words as long as I live. I've tried to follow this principle all my life and even pass it on to my children."

Coach Smith understood something about character: it's who you are when no one else is looking. Therefore, character is not determined by what others think of you, but by what you think of yourself.

I personally think Coach Smith is a person of outstanding character. This quality is fundamental for a great leader. Yes, Coach Smith has warts and human failures. There are certainly things in his life that, if he could do them over again differently, he would. Yet he is a man of tremendous integrity. A man of principle. A man of character.

Antoine de Saint-Exupery once said, "It is only with the heart one sees rightly. What is essential is invisible to the eye."

Coach Smith's invisible principles are what have helped bring him visible success. He always understood that there are no shortcuts to character, and he believed that if he lost his character, he would lose his credibility. We players instinctively followed him because we knew his words matched his life. We knew he was a person of high moral character. We sensed his humility, his compassion, and his care for us.

He never chose what was fashionable or easy over his character. He was always guided by doing what he felt was right, even when the critics decried him loudly and said the game had passed him by.

Leadership expert Stephen Covey wrote, "What is often missed in leadership is the character side. Without character, you can't have wisdom, in spite of competence. And without wisdom, you simply can't build and maintain an enduring institution, whether it be a marriage, a family, a team, or a company."

I believe there is a character crisis among leaders today. So many seem to be falling prey to the temptations of personal success and pleasure as their ultimate reasons for being in leadership. But before we can *do*, we must *be*. It's who we are when no one else is looking.

What are the character traits that have guided Coach Smith through the years? Let's look at some of them.

Leadership Principle Nine

Humility

When I asked Dean Smith what 879 wins represent to him, he quietly responded, "That I'm old."

Immediately after he broke Coach Rupp's record, he was interviewed on national television. He began to praise all the lettermen who had ever played for him. He really doesn't want the spotlight.

In fact, he hates interviews. He once told me, "I don't go out and talk on television after the games, except in the NCAA's. They make me do it or they kick you out of the NCAA. I prefer to send players out. I want them to be up front to the public."

John Lotz said that if you go to Coach Smith's home today you will not find any basketball memorabilia. That's very unusual for a successful leader in any field. "Oh, he is very aware of what he has accomplished and who he is," John said. "Yet he is also aware of all the people necessary for him to achieve all this. Therefore, personal exaltation seems inappropriate to him."

How many leaders would do this? Would they take the awards and commemorative photos off the walls to give evidence of all those who have helped them succeed?

In 1998 ESPN wanted to bestow upon Coach Smith the Arthur Ashe Award for courage, because of the many things he has done to promote racial equality in Chapel Hill and around the country. Smith did not want the award. He truly did not think he deserved it. Ashe's wife had to call him and ask him to receive the award on behalf of her husband and others who appreciated everything Coach Smith had done. He finally relented.

When he received the *Sports Illustrated* Sportsman of the Year Award for 1997, he demonstrated his customary humility. He named others he thought to be more deserving. Then, surprisingly, upon receiving the award he referred to Roland Thornqvist, a player on UNC's tennis team who did something amazing when he was about to win an important match. Smith said, "The referee made a bad call and gave him a point to win the nationals. He had it won, but he said, 'My shot was out.' He wouldn't accept it. He went onto win, but those kinds of guys are Sportsmen of the Year."

Dean Smith's humility illustrates something Stephen Covey wrote. "One of the characteristics of authentic leaders," Covey said, "is their humility, evident in their ability to take off their glasses and examine the lens objectively, analyzing how well their values, perceptions, beliefs, and behaviors align with 'true north' principles" (a term Covey uses to describe unchangeable principles that should shape every leader's life).

Covey went on to say that "as people become increasingly principle-centered, they love to share recognition and power." That aptly describes Coach Smith. He believed that if the team won, there should be enough recognition for the team. He hated the personal adulation, yet he would patiently sign autographs for anyone who wanted one. He simply believed that the more he refused to seek praise, the more that was left for the players. Remember what he said? "Players win games. I lose them."

Roy Williams, a former assistant and now coach of the very successful Kansas program, said, "Every time you talk to him, he starts trying to deflect his success to his team, his players, his assistants — the janitors." Talking about the phenomenal record of 879 wins, Williams said, "This record is a situation where the attention has to be focused on him...I think every player who's ever played at Carolina wanted it for him at least a thousand times more than the man wanted it himself."

When Smith announced his retirement, many of his former players gathered to support him. The championship trophies were all lined up behind him. Everything around him should have reminded him of his extraordinary success. Yet how did he respond? I think he did something very courageous. He shrugged his shoulders at his success and then gently chided the many reporters and the thousands of television viewers. He scolded them about total obsession with sports and winning.

As he reflected on the human condition worldwide, he could not reconcile it with the adulation being poured on him for simply winning basketball games. He said that if a Nobel prize-winning professor had just retired from UNC, hardly anyone would have noticed. It would not have begun to approach the fanfare of his retirement.

Any intelligent person knows Dean Smith is right. He simply has the courage, the principles, and the humility to state it.

Then, he started thanking all those with whom he had been associated through the years, especially his former players, for his success. Upon mentioning the former players, he began to cry.

A penetrating question for all leaders to ask is this: do I desire to receive the praise personally, or do I sincerely desire my employees to receive it? Someone once said that anything is attainable if we don't care who receives the credit. In a corporate climate of downsizing, where CEOs are jumping out of corporations with their golden parachutes and workers are left in anxiety wondering if they even have a job, humility would seem to be an important personal virtue for every leader.

Indira Gandhi summed up this perspective well. "My grandfather once told me," she said, "that there are two kinds of people: those who do the work and those who take the credit. He told me to try to be in the first group; there was less competition there."

I believe Coach Smith is in the first group. Most effective leaders are.

The church I oversee has grown and recently faced a multi-million-dollar building expansion. I inwardly struggled about spending so much on a building while there are so many needs in the world. So, naturally, I sought Coach Smith's counsel. After all, the University of North Carolina had built a 34-million-dollar basketball facility in 1986 and put Coach Smith's name on it. I wanted to know how he dealt with this.

When I asked him about it, a sheepish look crossed his face. He quickly responded, "I didn't like it one bit. I didn't want it and objected to it in every way. But they were determined. Frankly, it embarrasses me." It doesn't embarrass me or any other athlete who played for him. We think it's richly deserved and needed to be done in his lifetime to honor him. But he was genuinely embarrassed by how much money was spent. He said, "I wish all the players who played here for me could have their names on the building. That would be more fitting."

John Kilgo, editor of the UNC sports publication named *Carolina Blue,* shared with me how he witnessed the struggle Coach Smith felt internally during fundraising for the construction of the Smith Center. "He went with Skipper Bowles, a well-known UNC alumnus, when they were asking people for money. The plan was to double-team potential donors. Skipper knew how to raise money. Dean was the name.

"They went into the office of this multi-millionaire and started talking about the new building. The guy turned to Dean and said, 'Well, Coach, how much money do you need from me?' Dean became very uncomfortable. He wondered if the man thought he was giving the money to him personally, or giving just because Dean was asking.

"Dean asked tentatively, 'Would ten thousand dollars be okay? If you could give that, well, that would be sensational.'

"Skipper excused himself and took Dean into the hall. 'Next time,' he said, 'do everything you just did, but when the guy asks how much he can give, you be quiet and give it back to me. I'll take over.'

"So they went back into the office and Skipper asked the guy to please ask the question again about how much money he should give. The guy did and Skipper then asked for one and a half million dollars. The guy gave one million, but Dean still felt like ten thousand would have been more than enough. At that point, I think Skipper committed to leave Dean at home when asking others for contributions to the construction of the Smith Center. It simply made him too uncomfortable to ask for it."

Receiving Dean Smith's permission to have his name placed on the building was an equally daunting task. Several influential people kept pressing him for approval. He steadfastly refused. Finally, someone was smart enough to get some of the former players to approach him. They knew that only members of "the family" could ever convince him to change his mind. So several players went to him and asked him to accept this acknowledgment on behalf of every player who had ever played for him. That was the trump card. He finally agreed, for our sake, not his.

Hard Work

A successful mega-church pastor once told me about a young, aggressive seminarian who asked him the secret to his success.

The pastor quietly asked, "You really want to know the reason for my success?"

The seminarian enthusiastically nodded yes.

The pastor went over to his window, looked outside, and closed the shades. Then he went to the door, opened it and looked outside to see if anyone was looking. He called the seminarian to his side. In a hushed whisper, he said, "You want to know the reason for my success? Here it is: hard work."

Will Rogers once said, "Even if you're on the right track, you'll soon get run over if you just sit there."

Much of the reason for Coach Smith's success is that he simply out-worked and out-hustled his opponents. Yes, he was a great teacher and coach. Yes, he recruited well and had superb talent. Yes, he could moti-vate. But he also worked very hard.

For example, right after winning the national championship in 1993, he was in Rasheed Wallace's home the next day, enthusiastically — and successfully — recruiting him to play at North Carolina. Coach Smith was able to function on a few hours' sleep per night. He spent countless hours watching game films. He never lost a recruit because someone else worked harder. He always modeled a strong work ethic.

Personal Appearance and Conduct

John Ashcroft, senator from Missouri, was a guest on my weekly radio program on WBT here in Charlotte. He had recently written a book about lessons he had learned from his father. He said, "Concerning my appearance, dad always taught me daily to dress as if I were dressing for my next job."

Coach Smith demanded the same from us. When on the road, he demanded we dress nicely. In my days at UNC, it was in uniform, with a Carolina blue blazer and similar pants. He thought our outward appear-ance was extremely important, that it communicated something about what we thought of ourselves.

Woody Durham, the veteran voice of the Tar Heels, once did a tele-vision interview with Bob McAdoo, former UNC All-American in the early 1970s, outside of Carmichael Auditorium. "He had on one of those knit berets that was the rage," Durham said. "Coach Smith was pulling out of Carmichael to go some place. He suddenly stopped, interrupted the interview, and whispered something into McAdoo's ear. I quickly figured out what he said to McAdoo: take off the beret for the interview. McAdoo immediately obeyed."

When I interviewed Matt Doherty, now head coach at Notre Dame, he did not know I was doing an ancillary video piece. When he saw the camera as we started the interview, the first thing he did was apologize to Coach Smith for not wearing a tie and not using a good razor to get a close shave for the video. Coach Smith's message that personal appearance says something important for us publicly was a message that Doherty clearly understood!

In addition to teaching us to present a good image by dressing appropriately, Coach Smith insisted that our words reflect our character. He had a very strict rule about not cursing.

Was this a silly personal principle of integrity to emphasize? After all, cursing has become terribly common in our society. I played under Coach Smith for four years. In all that time I cannot remember one time I ever heard profanity from him.

Michael Jordan said, "No cursing. Yeah, I still remember that. You got to run the steps if you cursed. I had to run the steps a couple of times."

Phil Ford told me, "I never heard him curse at me, but sometimes I wish he had!" I knew what he meant. Sometimes his glare of disapproval was worse than a tongue-lashing.

I believe a couple of principles guided his thinking about bad language. It wasn't necessarily because of his rather strict Baptist upbringing, although I'm certain that did influence this area of his life. Nor is he prudish, self-righteous, or judgmental. To the contrary, he is one of the most accepting, gracious men I know.

I believe he did not curse nor allow us to curse because he wanted the best for us and himself. Dean Smith is an extremely bright man. When he entered the University of Kansas, he scored in the ninety-seventh percentile in math. In fact, Coach Guthridge says this may need to be the first thing people address when looking at Coach Smith's life. He is extremely intelligent, perhaps bordering on brilliant. Therefore, cursing for him represented an inadequate vocabulary — he told me he scored in the lower percentile in the verbal test! I think he strives to be the best he can be in anything he tackles, including his speech. For him, cursing represents a denigration of speech, an inadequacy of vocabulary he refuses to tolerate.

Second, I believe he wanted a similar excellence of speech from us. While I was in his office, he expressed disappointment in a former player's recent book, which contained some profanity. He was pleased with the book, but disdained the language. Cursing represented a poverty of vocabulary, and he wanted the best for himself and his players. Do we as leaders desire this same kind of excellence in our own personal appearance and our speech from those who work with us?

I've already related to you my close call with Coach Smith regarding his insistence on punctuality. He felt that being tardy was stealing — stealing another person's time. It didn't matter who you were, superstar or sub, if you weren't on time, there would be a consequence. He knew bosses wouldn't tolerate it later on, and he felt he needed to teach it now.

Woody Durham tells this story. "I remember one of the first times we went to Princeton. I was doing his TV show. He and I flew together, and we went to the hotel in time to catch the bus to practice. But the hotel clerk accidentally gave me the wrong room key. I remember it vividly. We were at the Howard Johnson's on the New Jersey turnpike. I yelled at him that I still had to get another key, and to have the bus wait for me because I'd just be a second. But when I walked outside to get on the bus, it was gone. He wouldn't wait for the president of the United States."

Donald Williams was almost late for the pre-game meal in the 1993 championship game. When he arrived Coach Smith said, "You're eight seconds ahead of the time limit." Williams, of course, started the game and was the hero, one of the prime reasons Carolina won the national championship. However, if he had been one second late, he would not have started the national championship game. And it was his watch that determined tardiness!

Is this a silly rule? Is it the dictates of a control freak? Or is it a key principle of a man who knows how the world operates and is committed to making young men into people of character? I think it is the latter.

I also demand that staff people be on time for meetings. I once had an intern who had an especially hard time doing this. I kept pushing him. Later I found out he told someone else that he did not have a positive experience on our staff because he always had to be on time. He failed to understand the importance of punctuality. He also struggled with it as he moved on to another job.

Are we leaders committed to teaching our underlings, especially younger ones, the value of punctuality? Do we believe we are stealing someone's time when we're late?

Honesty and Integrity

Another character trait that causes Dean Smith to stand out from the crowd is his absolute refusal to cheat. His unfailing honesty and integrity truly set him apart.

Andrew Carnegie once said, "As I grow older, I pay less attention to what men say. I just watch what they do." If you watch Coach Smith for a long time, you'll see that his words match up with his deeds in all of life's situations.

The dictionary defines integrity as "the state of being complete, unified." The opposite of integrity is duplicity and hypocrisy.

When I was a senior in high school, Coach Smith came down to Orlando, Florida, to recruit me. We went to eat at a well-known eating establishment at the Orlando airport; it happened to be owned and operated by one of my father's close friends.

When we finished our meal, Coach Smith asked for the check. My dad's friend came to the table and said dinner was on the house. Coach Smith objected. Dad's friend insisted. Coach Smith objected even more vociferously. The resistance continued.

Finally, Coach Smith said that this could be breaking NCAA rules and he could not permit it. My dad's friend finally yielded. This story shows how Smith was able to coach for 35 years and not once have the smell of scandal taint his program. Honesty was an absolutely essential life principle for him.

Coach Guthridge gave me another illustration that demonstrates the same truth. If Coach Smith ever played golf with someone who cheated — moved their ball unfairly in the rough, inched the ball a bit closer on the green — he would simply walk off the golf course and never play with that person again. He demanded honesty from himself and those around him. He was not a cheater and he refused to play with one. Roy Williams told me that unless the golf ball is hanging on the edge of the hole, Dean Smith will make you putt it out. "He would always say, 'How do I know you can make that putt? Make it and prove to me you're a good golfer.'"

Coach Smith steadfastly refused to cheat. He made that decision before he ever accepted the job as head coach at North Carolina. When he was hired, the chancellor told him to run a clean program and recruit able scholar-athletes. Winning was not the highest priority. Therefore, the decision to cheat was never a temptation. But I don't think it had to be. His own personal character would not allow him to cheat under any circumstances.

I must admit some incredulity about this. How could a contemporary coach win and *not* cheat? So I asked John Swofford, the athletic director over Coach Smith for 17 years, if it were true that Smith never cheated. He replied, "Nothing you could put in the category of cheating at all. You know, if you've ever looked at the NCAA rule book, and the thickness of it, there are all kinds of things on which you could stub your toe. But anytime there was a question at North Carolina in terms of a violation, we would turn it into the NCAA immediately. We were never investigated. Nothing of any substance was ever unearthed. That's because of Dean's absolute commitment to run a clean program."

Eddie Fogler, present coach at the University of South Carolina, offered this perspective. "Even though he had intense rivalries, I don't think any opposing coach would ever believe that Dean Smith would violate an NCAA rule. He is that well thought of among his peers. They know his integrity and honesty. That is the way he has always done it.

"One thing that especially bothered him was the suggestion that he didn't have to recruit players, that he could simply select the ones he wanted. He often interpreted that to mean that if his teams weren't good, or if he didn't coach at a great school, that perhaps he would cheat. Well, Coach Smith could be at the worst school at the bottom of the best conference and there is no way he would ever violate NCAA rules. If he lost his job because of his refusal to cheat, then he would lose his job."

I asked Swofford if this commitment to honesty positively influenced other parts of the athletic program. "Of course!" he responded quickly. "The way he ran the basketball program had a tremendous influence on the rest of the athletic program. He set the standard of integrity. Because of his commitment to academics over athletics, his incredible graduation rate, the way his players loved him, the way he treated people, and his refusal to cheat, he set the bar for the other departments. In fact, whenever we interviewed a coach in another sport, we would point to the basketball program as an example of what can be done and how we want it to be done. I used his extraordinary honesty and success to challenge other divisions. Not only did it work, but it produced an excellence among us all. It's one of, if not the major reason we regularly won the nation's all-sports trophy."

Woody Durham even suggested that Coach Smith's overwhelming commitment to honesty may have been one of the reasons he ultimately retired. When I asked him to explain, he said, "There is such a huge commitment by Coach Smith to play by the rules. He would never counsel his big men, even if they were 6'9" and weighed 270 pounds, to use their strength wrongly if it were against the rules."

One of the most publicized encounters Coach Smith ever had with a rival coach was with Rick Barnes (who was then at Clemson, now Texas) in the opening round of the ACC Tournament a few years ago. A Clemson player had undercut UNC superstar Jerry Stackhouse. Coach Smith went after the player and Coach Barnes. From Coach Smith's standpoint, I think it had little to do with protecting his players, as the press suggested. It had nothing to do, in my opinion, with a personal vendetta against Rick Barnes. It had everything to do with the way Coach Smith thought the game should be played. When the Clemson player undercut Stackhouse, yes, Coach Smith was concerned with Stackhouse's well-being. But he was much more concerned with the game not being played the way the rules stated.

"He sincerely regretted the confrontation after it happened," Durham told me. "But he was saying to the official and everyone, 'Hey, there are rules, a book, and a way the game is supposed to be played. This is not the way the game was designed to be played.'"

Reflecting on Coach Smith's love for the way the game should be played and how it had changed over the years, Durham concluded, "I think he became frustrated that the rules were not being followed, and it helped motivate him to retire."

Leaders, is honesty important to you? Is being above reproach essential to your leadership? Will you refuse to deal with anyone who bends or breaks the rules to succeed? Parents teach their children that honesty is the best policy. Coach Smith believed and practiced this maxim at all times.

Learning How to Be Under Authority

Before I began my ministry, I had the privilege of visiting with a prominent person in religious circles. Desiring success, I asked him what I needed to do first to pave my path to personal achievement. His answer surprised me. He said, "Go serve in someone else's ministry. Learn how to help him succeed. Learn how to be under authority. Then you'll be ready for success."

Actually, that's sound advice for any endeavor. You can benefit from being a student of someone else's experience, picking up not only technical skills and knowledge in your field, but an understanding of what it takes to be a leader.

Coach Smith understood what it meant to be under authority. As athletic director, John Swofford was Coach Smith's boss. I asked him if Coach Smith ever caused him problems. He quickly retorted, "Absolutely not!

"He respected my position," he continued. "Very successful coaches can make athletic directors' lives miserable, wielding such power and influence over alumni and others that our lives can be in constant chaos. This was never the case with Dean. He respected proper lines of authority.

"Whenever we disagreed, or he disagreed with the chancellor, it was always behind closed doors. We did have our disagreements, although not many of consequence. But you can imagine, at this level, there were times when I had to make decisions with which he didn't agree. How did he handle it? He was always respectful. Sometimes he would be forceful in his opinions, as I would hope he would be. However, when he left my office, he would either actively support the decision publicly or never state his opposition to it. He would never give negative publicity or the indication there was disunity. He was a person who understood what it meant to submit to authority."

Perhaps Coach Smith learned this principle from being an assistant under Bob Spear at the Air Force Academy and Frank McGuire at North Carolina. For example, no one can remember Coach Smith ever asserting himself against McGuire; he was completely loyal to him. In fact, during the years when McGuire's South Carolina teams were North Carolina's most fierce rivals, Coach Smith would always ask North Carolina fans to heartily and respectfully welcome McGuire back to Chapel Hill.

Or perhaps he took a page from Nordstrom's, which demands that every new worker starts at the bottom. If you're not willing to do whatever it takes to make a customer happy at the lowest level, from delivering a suit to a hotel room to getting on your knees to fit a shoe, you'll never be a leader in the organization.

However he learned it, Dean Smith understood that the best leader is the one who has learned to be under authority. I learned this truth through the most difficult time of my leadership. When I took this church through a new vision, it was very painful. People were highly critical. Some actually left the church. I shared in an earlier chapter that the healing of this very painful experience began when I went before the entire congregation, asked for forgiveness, and then began to build leadership consensus behind the scenes.

What I did not share, however, is what happened to lead up to that decision to go before the congregation. I was in a logjam with my lay leadership. I felt we should go in one direction. They simply weren't sure. I went away for a couple of weeks of vacation, confused about what I should do. My view of leadership at that point was that I was the leader, I received the vision, and they should follow. But it wasn't working. In fact, it was only alienating my lay leadership from me.

I then read a little book that said effective leaders in the twenty-first century will be people who have learned to submit to others and trust that the group can reach the right decision together. At first, I balked at the suggestion. How could I trust lay people to understand the right direction for the church? I was the one spending most all my time there.

They were only part-time. But the more I considered it, the more I knew the author was correct. I therefore decided to be a person under authority, to trust the process and believe that they, too, had the best interests of the church at heart.

I returned from my vacation. We scheduled our first meeting together. Tension filled the air. The lay leadership anxiously wanted to know what I would say. Finally, I told them about my time away and the book I had read. I told them I wanted to trust the process. I said, "I want to hear where you think the church should go. I am submitting to your wisdom." There was a stunned silence. That was not what they were expecting from me. They thought there would be more battles to fight. But it takes two to fight, and I had eliminated myself from the struggle.

What happened next was absolutely amazing. After several moments of stunned silence, one of the most influential leaders finally said, "Well, David, where again do you think we ought to go?" They gave me back my leadership. When I submitted to their authority, I was given authority in return. And we began together to hammer out the vision that, interestingly, was almost exactly the one I felt was right for the church. They were the ones who counseled me to appear before the congregation, apologize for my mistakes, and begin to work for consensus.

Leaders, when is the last time you willingly submitted to those over you? Did you publicly support the decision or pout? Did you seek unity above all else?

The Leader as Servant

Peter Drucker once said, "No leader is worth his salt who won't set up chairs." He meant that leaders who won't serve can't lead. Ken Blanchard, chairman of Blanchard Leadership and Training, and a popular author on leadership, had a similar view of customer service. "Customers are treated as if they really are the most important part of the business. Every employee and manager seeks to serve the customer or support those who do."

People are Coach Smith's most important product. He was and is extremely loyal to his players. He seeks to serve them. What many people don't know about Coach Smith, however, is how he has tried to care for many people he didn't even know. For example, my father was talking to the man painting my parents' house. Dad mentioned the book I was writing. The man then proceeded to tell about his father, a huge Carolina fan, who died of cancer. Coach Smith had learned of his condition, and one day while in Charlotte, he dropped by this man's hospital room unannounced. He brought a couple of players with him. For several minutes he cared for this fan, expressing genuine concern about his condition. The painter told my father, "He'll never know what that meant to my dad."

Coach Smith sees leadership as being a servant and putting others' needs first.

Equality for All

John Lotz thinks that a deep belief in equality motivated practically everything Dean Smith did, whether it was a religious, political, or athletic conviction. For example, the reason he treated the twelfth man on the team the same as the superstar is his belief that all people are created equal.

Coach Smith has been a champion for the cause of racial equality. Bill Chamberlain, one of the first African-American players recruited at Carolina, told me that even today when he becomes angry with racial inequality in America, he writes Coach Smith, sometimes just to get it off his chest. Every time he has written, Coach Smith replies, sensitively listening, encouraging Chamberlain to look at it from another perspective, or empathizing with his anguish.

In 1959 Coach Smith and his pastor took an African-American seminary student and sat down in a Chapel Hill whites-only restaurant. It was the first step toward serious integration in Chapel Hill. When asked about it, Coach Smith simply said, "It was the right thing to do."

Coach Smith recruited Charlie Scott, the first Carolina black athlete, in 1966. A year later Smith followed by recruiting Chamberlain, his second black player. Not until 1970 did Coach Adolph Rupp allow a black player on his team.

It was Coach Smith who asked John Thompson, a dear friend with a darker skin hue, to be his assistant coach for the gold-medal-winning USA Olympic team in 1976.

And it is Coach Smith who continually asks if the SAT is racially biased.

This commitment to equality, however, transcended his passion for racial justice. Everyone on the team, from the manager to the superstar, was treated fairly on and off the court, before and after graduation.

Donn Johnston, 1968–1972 letterman, is a Philadelphia lawyer who specializes in executive benefits and financial planning. He wrote to me, "I continue to use all of Coach Smith's principles on a daily basis. For example, treating everyone equally. It is very easy to focus attention on the individuals who bring business to the organization: the superstars. It is important for all to know there would be no superstars without those who work behind the scenes generating proposals, getting products out the door on a timely basis, and keeping the client happy when service issues arise. It is important to make these individuals part of the team and to demonstrate that their contributions are appreciated."

Leaders, do you see everyone in your organization as being created equally? How do you express your commitment to this principle beyond what the government demands? Do you show favoritism, partisanship? Has it destroyed your work environment yet?

Compassion for All

In the late 1980s Dean Smith spoke at a banquet I helped organize to raise money for an inner-city scholarship program. He hates to do that kind of thing. But he did. Was it because I was a former player and asked him to do it? Perhaps, yet he has turned me down on other offerings. I think he did it for one reason: it was a ministry to the poor.

Few will ever know his deep conviction to help the poorest of the poor. Heaven only knows how much time and money he has given to people and causes around the world to help clothe and feed the hungry and homeless. James Worthy said, "I remember receiving a unique Christmas present from him once. He sponsored a child in another country in my name. That really touched me."

Each Christmas my staff tries to discover a need among the poor of the world. We share this with our kids. We tell them that we may not have as many gifts under the tree because we want to help others in dire need. It has been a wonderful experience, keeping us in tune with the needs of others and helping us not be ungrateful and self-absorbed. We also ask each staff member to remember the poor throughout the year with special gifts and involvement. Several regularly go downtown to the soup kitchen to remind us of this responsibility.

If leaders only live in their nice homes without any reflection on the needs of the world, they most certainly will become hardened to hurts. Inevitably, that must be reflected in the workplace.

Coach Smith's generosity to the less fortunate extends far beyond an occasional project. It's more of a way of life for him; he is simply not money driven.

Carolina basketball teams travel first class on commercial flights or on planes chartered from NBA teams. They dine in fine restaurants and stay in the best hotels. But the team can afford to travel first class. The basketball program took in 7.2 million dollars last year and cost just 2.8 million to run.

Yet all this began to gnaw at Coach Smith. "I got to worrying that we were telling the players the wrong things by always staying in the best hotels or eating the biggest steak," he said. "I asked the players, 'Are we giving you the wrong message about materialism?'"

Smith was embarrassed by how much money he made — $162,750 in salary in 1997 before his retirement. When North Carolina signed a $4.7-million, four-year deal with Nike in 1993, Coach Smith made sure it covered 24 of the school's teams, although the athletic director said "this easily could have been a contract just for Coach Smith."

He received $500,000 from Nike as an up-front gift. Did he take it all and vault himself into the upper echelon of coaches' compensation? No! He gave away half of his annual $300,000 Nike salary, distributing it among his assistants and office staff. He also earmarked $45,000 of his annual salary for a special fund to be used by players who had yet to finish their degrees. He is even concerned for the three percent of his players who haven't graduated!

When John Kilgo hosted the Dean Smith Show on television, many businesses would approach him to ask him to convince Coach Smith to endorse their products. They would say, "He doesn't have to make a statement. We just want his picture alongside our product, and we will pay him a huge amount of money." Kilgo took these different offers to Coach Smith. Repeatedly he turned them down.

"But every other coach is doing it!" John said.

Coach Smith replied, "The professors on this campus would not be comfortable with the school's basketball coach making that much money doing something like that. I consider myself a teacher and it wouldn't be fair to receive that kind of money. It would send the wrong message."

Kilgo went on to say that Coach Smith made about one-tenth of what he could have made at North Carolina. All these opportunities were legitimate. "I kept pointing out to him that if the professors, even the chancellor, had an opportunity to do this, they would. But he wouldn't do it. He not only didn't want to make this kind of money, but he thought it was gross that anybody else did!"

When I asked Dave Hanners about Coach Smith's disdain for money and his silent generosity to those in need, he said, "Money is of no importance to him. He only drives a BMW because someone gave it to him. He doesn't care. I wish people knew how many times and for how many people, especially his former players, he has written personal checks to bail them out of trouble. I believe with all my heart that the only reason he desired to make any money at all was so he could give it away and help somebody else."

Terry Truax was a graduate assistant in the UNC program in 1971. He later was an assistant with John Lotz at the University of Florida, and subsequently became head coach at Towson State University, guiding them to the NCAA tournament on a couple of occasions.

Ultimately, Truax was let go from Towson. Between jobs, money was tight. One day, completely unannounced, came a check in the mail for $5000. It was from Coach Smith. A note was attached to the check saying that Smith had been unable to pay Truax much back in 1971. Now that he had some means, Coach Smith wanted to give the money to Truax in repayment for all his hard work at UNC years earlier.

As the cover story of *Newsweek* in February 1996 suggests, there's a struggle between lay-offs and CEO's salaries. Among the 12 corporations featured, 363,800 jobs were eliminated while the 12 CEOs together pocketed $19,736,011, not including stock options and benefits. What's wrong with this picture? Does this foster support or resentment? Doesn't resentment then pass over the remaining workers like the sword of Damocles? Isn't profit imperceptibly hurt even more in the long run?

Leaders, do you consider profit the means to the end or the end itself? Shouldn't money be the means to help people, who are indeed life's most precious commodity and important product? How does your salary compare with those who work with you? Is it highly unequal? Does this disparity create disunity?

A concern for the poor is not Coach Smith's only social concern. He has asked the NCAA to explore the integrity of having beer companies fund games and tournaments. With teenage alcoholism rampant and drunk drivers killing people by the thousands, in his opinion it's a bad image for college athletics to be associated with alcohol-related sponsors.

His wife Linnea, a psychiatrist, has asked Carolina preseason All-Americans to refuse to be a part of *Playboy's* preseason picture of its All-American team. Coach Smith agrees. He thinks the magazine degrades women, and this is one way he can protest.

Coach Smith would be the last person to try and impose his beliefs on another person. He would say these social causes are very important concerns for him. However, I think he would challenge us all to see ourselves as a part of a larger community, to look at ways we can be a part of the larger good, individually and corporately.

Conviction Above Convenience

Perhaps the character trait of Coach Smith's that I admire most is his willingness to express his convictions no matter what the consequences may be. One of his firm convictions is that freshmen athletes should be barred from varsity sports so they can concentrate first on their academics. He believes athletes go to college to be students.

Smith opposed the rule change in 1972 that allowed freshmen to play varsity sports. When this change occurred, the competition for high school athletes intensified. Recruiting now begins in junior high school. This change also communicated to athletes the lie that college is a training ground for professional sports. Yet fewer than one percent of high school players get college scholarships, and fewer than one in a thousand go on to become professionals. In fact, most never even complete their degrees and consequently have nothing on which to fall back.

Coach Smith made the audacious proposal to permit freshmen to receive scholarships even if they sat out the first year altogether, allowing them to adjust to campus life and the rigors of academia. Then he proposed that these freshmen continue to receive full financial scholarship aid as they advance toward their degree.

Naturally, the dissenters say that the cost of this would be much too great. Yet this argument seems spurious when you think about the millions being generated by college athletics. For example, the major bowls are paying an average of eight million dollars to the teams and conferences playing in bowl games. Most schools are against the proposed rule because if they can recruit one great player, he can turn the entire program around.

Coach Smith furiously argues that part of the money made by these universities could be used to support freshmen athletes adjusting to academia. As he put it, "We would be saying, 'You're here as a student first. Once you've shown us your ability as a student, we'd be happy to have you as an athlete too.'" What's so interesting is Coach Smith and UNC would have been one of the nation's teams to benefit least from freshmen ineligibility. Since they were always getting commitments from the best high school players who would help the program immediately, to ask for freshmen ineligibility would certainly hurt UNC more than most other programs. But that wasn't the point. Coach Smith had strong convictions and they always held over convenience.

After Coach Smith retired, Bernie Linicome of the *Chicago Tribune* wrote: "He has been my coach...and everyone else's too, if they bothered to have one. It is not so much what he was — an innovator, if you count the Four-Corners offense, a tactic that once allowed North Carolina to beat Duke 21–20 — but it is what he wasn't. He was not a bully, he was not a cheat, and he was not a liar, the three items that lead the resume of most college coaches."

Dean Smith did it the right way, not with rage but with resolve, not with payoffs but with patience, not with intimidation but with inspiration.

Money, success, victory, and fame simply don't drive him. His conviction of character does.

Recruiting Character

Because of his own commitment to character, Coach Smith tried to recruit young men who also had character. He wanted good athletes, but he also wanted to recruit good people.

"We did look at a young man's character," he told me. "Indeed, if I had to do it over again, I think that would be even a bigger factor. I would not be so much concerned with his beliefs, but I would watch closely for his willingness to work hard, his tenacity to stay with a difficult situation.

"I probably would be willing to recruit more people like Hubert Davis. I told his dad he could maybe play for George Washington. Then he came here and was a first-round draft pick in the NBA. Sometimes we saw a player's court demeanor and walked away from him. There were probably some others in whom I saw potential problems but took them anyway because of their ability. Life is too short. I would probably make character an even higher priority in recruiting if I were doing it today."

How did he discover if a player had character? James Worthy revealed one of his secrets. "I was a blue chipper," Worthy said. "A lot of colleges wanted me. When Coach Smith came to visit me, I was wondering about playing time, if I was going to be a star, and if I'd get a pair of sneakers. The only thing he said to me is that I'd have to go to class unless I had a written permission slip from my parents. I also had to go to church each Sunday. 'That is what we do at Carolina,' he said.

"Later I realized he was recruiting character. He was looking for good players and good people. He knew these kinds of kids best played his philosophy."

Not only did he spend a lot of time with the parents on recruiting visits, but he would also watch a player's interaction with his parents. Did he show respect, for example? I imagine that while he spent so much time talking with James Worthy's parents, he was watching James's reaction. Was he irritated that Coach Smith wasn't speaking to him?

He also spent much time with a player's high school coaches. He valued their input on character. During games he closely watched how a recruit played — was he selfish or unselfish? — and how he spoke to officials, coaches, and teammates.

Perhaps the best example I could give of Coach Smith's ability to recruit character would be Bill Guthridge, his long-time assistant and eventual successor. Coach Smith gave the same detailed attention to recruiting assistants as he did players, and when he recruited Coach Guthridge, he made an outstanding choice.

The Charlotte Observer did a feature article on Coach Guthridge right after North Carolina won the ACC Tournament in March 1998. The article described Coach Guthridge's narrow escape from polio at age 11. Medical tests showed he had the virus but recovered quickly. One of his neighbors, a boy who lived four houses down, was not so fortunate:

> One morning when he was twelve, Bob Brandenburg didn't feel much like playing. The next morning he couldn't get out of bed.
>
> It could be devastatingly fast, polio.
>
> By the time school started in the fall, Brandenburg was in a wheelchair. The junior high was about one hundred yards away, up a slight incline. That first morning, as he looked out the window at the kids moving past, Brandenburg saw someone waiting in the driveway.
>
> Guthridge had come to push him to school.
>
> "I'd had polio a year earlier, so I could empathize," Guthridge says. "I think anybody would have been happy to help."
>
> "Bill was such a loyal person," Brandenburg says. "He pushed me to school the next six years."

Leonard Bernstein, the famous orchestral conductor, was once asked what was the most difficult instrument to play in the orchestra. Without blinking an eye he responded, "Second fiddle." Coach Guthridge loyally played second fiddle to Coach Smith for more than 30 years. But he had demonstrated his loyalty much earlier by pushing a friend's wheelchair for six years.

John Lotz, another long-time assistant in the 1960s and 1970s, also understood that Coach Smith recruited character in his assistants. "When he approached me about coming on staff, he knew the quality of my life. He knew my background and my character. He wanted someone to help recruit good student-athletes and be loyal to him. I enjoyed being that person, because I knew his character and knew that he would be loyal to me."

Dean Smith knew how to find players and coaches with sterling character. It's a valuable skill for a leader to learn, because recruiting character can make a tremendous difference in a positive work environment and production.

Thought for the Day

Before we can do, we must be.

Game Plan

- Humility

- Hard work

- Honesty and integrity

- Personal appearance and conduct

- Submitting to authority

- The leader as servant

- Equality for all

- Compassion for all

- Convictions above convenience

- Recruiting character

Team Practice

- How do you demonstrate honesty in your personal life?

- How do you demonstrate honesty at work?

- What happens when your beliefs are different from the beliefs of others in your organization?

10

MAKING FAILURE
YOUR FRIEND

"Look at your mistake,
learn from it, and move on."

The 1994 team was supposed to be one of Carolina's best ever. Four starters returned from the 1993 national championship team, and three gifted freshmen — Jeff McInnis, Jerry Stackhouse, and Rasheed Wallace — joined the team. But the players never jelled as a team. They lost in the second round of the NCAA tournament to an undersized and undermanned Boston College team.

In preparation for the next year, Coach Smith sent his players a copy of the front page of *Sports Illustrated* after the Boston College upset. It was titled, "A Talented Team Falls Flat." In the accompanying article, the writer said, "Smith, whose greatness is undeniable, may have done the worst coaching job of his career with the most talent he has had."

Coach Smith was unafraid for the team to read this criticism. Indeed, he wanted them to see this failure. He then challenged this team to be better, vowing he would be a better coach. The team was very successful that season.

I had originally decided not to write this chapter as a part of this book. Yet the more I though about all Coach Smith had taught me about life and leadership, it became increasingly apparent that I would be remiss if I failed to include it.

In fact, after I had almost completed the manuscript, I went to Chapel Hill to update him on the project. During our meeting, I mentioned that I wanted to write about making failure your friend. His response was immediate: "Please do it. That's a very important principle for me."

As we visited, Coach Smith recalled a particular day in practice when Matt Wenstrom did something wrong, and then started to pout.

Coach Smith went over to him and asked, "How do you handle mistakes in life?"

Wenstrom quickly recited the thought for the day from the practice plan. "When faced with failure, recognize it, admit it, learn from it, forget it!"

Coach said to all the players, "If you can learn any one thing in life, learn that! Learn from your mistakes and move on."

Someone once said, "You don't drown by falling in the water. You drown by staying there!"

Coach Smith's career was marked by many failures. But he continued to learn from them. He steadfastly refused to stay in the water and drown. Instead, he learned how to become a fantastic swimmer.

A question often posed at leadership and management training seminars is, "Are leaders born or made?" The answer must be, "both."

Leaders must be born with an innate intelligence and giftedness to lead. Coach Guthridge ventured his opinion on why Coach Smith was so successful. "What few people ever talk about is the fact that Coach Smith is an extremely intelligent person. So when you factor together his intelligence with hard work and preparation, and then learning from different failures in life, well, that equals a very successful coach and leader."

Leaders need an innate intelligence. However, we cannot miss Coach Guthridge's last comment that leaders must also learn from life's failures. Leaders are born...and made!

R.L. Johnson Jr., former CEO of Johnson and Johnson, profoundly stated, "Failure is our most important product." Indeed, its baby talc came about when Fred Kilmer, its director of research, responded to a physician's critical letter who complained about patient skin irritation from Johnson and Johnson's medical plasters. He simply sent the talc to soothe the skin and success was birthed!

Dean Smith learned many leadership skills in the fires of life's failure. We too often forget those early years, when he didn't win, when the critics said he would never win at college basketball's highest level.

We forget that students in Chapel Hill hung him in effigy in the early 1960s because he didn't win a big game. We forget that alumni wanted him dismissed during those early seasons.

We forget that for two decades critics said he couldn't win the big one, the national championship. When he finally did win it in 1982, they said, amazingly, that he probably couldn't do it again.

We forget that in the 1990s, before his second national championship in 1993, critics said the game had passed Dean Smith by and suggested he retire, allowing UNC to get a younger coach who could relate better to contemporary college players.

We forget that one rival ACC coach named his dog "Dean" because, the man said, "he cries and whines so much!"

We should remember all these things, because these failures and criticisms forged his character, strengthened his resolve, and forced him to grow as a leader. I think he knew that the fear of failure is the greatest enemy of success. Therefore, he learned to embrace failure. He learned to make failure his friend.

Tom Peters, the management consultant and best-selling author, urges us all to celebrate our failures, learn from them and, indeed, build on them. For him, failures are an essential part of progress. He said, "The essence of innovation is the pursuit of failure...to be able to make mistakes and not get shot."

He then quoted Soichiro Honda, the founder of the Japanese automobile of the same name, who said, "Many people dream of success. To me, success can only be achieved through repeated failure and introspection. In fact, success represents the one percent of your work which results only from ninety-nine percent that is called failure."

Or, as that inimitable philosopher, Dolly Parton, once said, "The way I see it, if you want the rainbow, you gotta put up with the rain."

Failure Does Not Have to Be a Foe

When we look at Coach Smith, the winningest coach in college basketball history, we tend to forget the losses. It's the same way with leaders in all walks of life.

The average American millionaire, for example, has been bankrupt 3.75 times. Henry Ford went broke on five different occasions before he finally succeeded.

Albert Einstein did not speak one word until he was four years old. He couldn't read until he was seven. One teacher described him as "mentally slow, unsociable, and adrift forever in his foolish dreams." Another called him "uneducable." The Zurich Polytechnic School refused him admittance.

The father of the famous sculptor, Rodin, once said to him, "I have an idiot for a son." His teachers described him as the worst pupil in the school. He failed three different times to gain entrance to the school of art.

Some of the world's most famous products were the results of mistakes: cheese, aspirin, paper towels, and penicillin, just to mention a few.

The man who dreamed up the photocopier thought he had discovered something wonderful to aid industry. He shopped his invention to IBM, Kodak, and RCA. They all scoffed at the idea and rejected it. Ready to give in to failure, he finally took the idea to Xerox. The rest is history. I can tell you that everyone on my office team appreciates the fact that he made failure his friend and didn't give up!

Dewitt and Lila Wallace had done a bit of everything from farming to DeWitt fighting and being wounded in World War I. He became a copywriter, but was fired. They finally came up with the idea of digesting much reading material into one magazine. They took the idea to several New York publishers. It was rejected by all.

So in 1921 they borrowed money and started the magazine in a small room beneath a speak-easy in Greenwich Village. More than three-quarters of a century later, *Reader's Digest* sells almost 28 million copies per month. For those of us with limited time, we're glad that the Wallaces made failure their friend.

Failure can be a leader's most formidable foe, but it doesn't have to be.

Walt Disney was abruptly dismissed by a newspaper editor for whom he worked. What was the reason for the dismissal? The editor said Disney lacked new, creative ideas. Disney was also personally bankrupt several times before he finally came up with the new, creative idea of Disneyland.

In fact, few know that Disney had an animation business in Kansas City, Missouri, that went under. That's what caused his move to California. So in 1923, at the ripe age of 22, he moved in with his uncle Robert in Hollywood. Rent was $5 for room and board. However, soon Disney ran out of money. His uncle's patience waned and he was ready to send Disney to the streets. At last, a vaudeville-house operator finally agreed to sponsor a cartoon series.

Disney then constructed a simple wooden box in his uncle's garage. The cartoons were quite simple, just stick figures with the jokes printed in comic-strip balloons. Yet that was the start of Walt Disney's cartoon genius, now reaping profits annually of $22.5 billion.

Boeing went through difficult struggles in the 1930s, 1940s, and again in the 1970s after it had to lay-off 60,000 employees. Hewlett Packard had severe cutbacks in 1945. In 1990, its stock value dropped below book value. Ford suffered one of America's largest annual losses in the early 1980s ($3.3 billion in three years) before it began a new core value of people first. IBM was nearly bankrupt in 1914 and 1921, and experienced difficulties again in the 1990s. Many great people and companies suffer failure; they just know how to make it a friend.

Madeleine L'Engle wrote a children's book titled *A Wrinkle in Time*. My own children have read it over and over again. It's one of their favorites. But the book was rejected by more than 50 publishers before seeing print.

Vince Lombardi once had an "expert" say this about him: "He possesses minimal football knowledge. He also lacks motivation." This expert predicted failure for Lombardi as a football coach.

Winston Churchill failed the sixth grade. He twice failed to achieve an elected office during the early 1920s and had little political influence all through the 1930s. But he learned from his failures and kept developing his talents. In 1940 he became prime minister of England at the age of 62. Today he is acclaimed as a great leader and hero of World War II. The free world is certainly glad he made failure his friend.

A young man named Rocko wanted to become a big league baseball player more than anything else in the world. For years he tried to develop his skills. Finally he took a long train ride to Fayetteville, North Carolina, for a try-out with a major league team. He hit one double, but other than that his performance was uneventful.

On the long train ride home he felt great disappointment and was ready to give up. He asked a friend riding the train with him about boxing; Rocko thought he could be successful in that sport. His friend, Ray Gormley, said Rocko had no future in boxing and discouraged him from trying.

Yet he did give boxing a try, and he became a world champion. Millions of fans knew him as Rocky Marciano.

The Greatest American Failure

"There lies the most perfect ruler of men the world has ever seen...and now he belongs to the ages."

Which great world leader did this statement address? Alexander the Great? Winston Churchill? Julius Caesar? George Patton? John F. Kennedy? No, none of these is right.

Perhaps some background information would help.

When he was seven years old, his family was evicted from their home because of a legal technicality. As a result, he was forced to go to work in order to help support them.

At age nine, while groping to find his identity as a child and suffering from extreme shyness, his mother died.

At 22, he lost his job as a store clerk. He was therefore unable to secure the proper education to fulfill his desire to attend law school.

At 23, he became a partner in a small business enterprise but went into huge debt when his partner died and left him the debt to repay.

At 28, he asked a young lady whom he had been dating for four years to marry him. She declined. This was the second romantic disappointment for the man. An earlier youthful relationship had tragically ended when his love died.

At 37, after three unsuccessful attempts, he was elected to Congress. Two years later he tried for re-election, but was defeated. It was during this time he had what contemporary psychologists call a nervous breakdown.

At 41, during the time when his marriage was aching, his four-year-old son died.

At 42, he applied to be a land officer. He was rejected.

At 45, he ran for the Senate and lost.

At 47, he was defeated for nomination as the vice president of the United States.

At 49, he ran for the Senate again…and was defeated again.

During these long years of disappointment, critics circulated false rumors about him. Consequently, he suffered from long, deep periods of depression.

Yet, at 51, he was elected president of the United States, only to have his second term in office cut short by an assassin's bullet.

While he was dying, one of his chief antagonists, Edwin Stanton, spoke the statement previously quoted: "There lies the most perfect ruler of men the world has ever seen…and now he belongs to the ages."

Abraham Lincoln, one of America's most inspirational and gifted leaders, could in many ways be considered the greatest American failure. Yet he knew the truth that pain can lead us to possibilities and suffering can lead to success. He, too, allowed failure to be his friend, and the United States is a better nation because of it.

Every outstanding leader knows this truth: we learn much more from our failures than from our successes. It is in the pain of failure that we gain new insights about our weaknesses and how to succeed. Adversity becomes life's university.

Learning from Mistakes

In my own most difficult leadership crisis, Coach Smith's words about making friends with failure proved invaluable. Let me give you some background. I have been the leader of Forest Hill Church for 19 years.

About six years ago, after turning down an opportunity to lead another congregation, I felt the time was right to move the church in another direction. We had grown significantly in previous years, but most of the growth had come from people dissatisfied with other churches. Simply receiving another organization's dissatisfied customers did not connote health. I felt that for a church to be truly outreach-oriented, it needed to make more efforts to reach the unchurched. Besides, the disgruntled people often brought their own baggage and hurts from their previous churches. Eventually, they became angry with us, too.

With this in mind, I wrote a 70-page position paper that I felt would direct us into the twenty-first century. Forty of this church's significant leaders gathered together for a weekend and I enthusiastically cast the new vision. There was some discussion. However, in my zeal, I committed a huge leadership mistake. Beginning the second day, I said something like, "Well, I believe so much in this new vision that if you don't want to do it, I may have to go somewhere else."

I'm sure, in retrospect, that's not what I intended to say. Moreover, I'm certain I was undergoing some "aging and staging" in my life. I was in my early forties and was subconsciously applying leadership pressure to myself and the other leaders so the new vision could happen as quickly as possible.

However, I failed to realize that the leadership of the church felt bullied. They sincerely respected me, but they still felt bullied. They didn't tell me what they were feeling, however. Maybe they didn't want to hurt my feelings. Maybe they didn't know how to tell me. At the end of the weekend, they gave unanimous support for the new vision, although I didn't recognize their unanswered concerns.

As I aggressively moved ahead, casting the vision at every opportunity, more and more people felt alienated and hurt. It took months before I finally realized it. The people in the church simply were not moving in step with me.

During the next several months, several staff members left. One became pregnant. Another felt called to return to seminary for more graduate work. I had to let another one go. Another suffered a massive heart attack and died. Suddenly I had four staff positions open. I also had a new vision to which to recruit new staff. And that's exactly what I did.

We recruited all over the country and tried to find the best people possible. Over the course of the next year, all four staff positions were filled with gifted, aggressive, and excited people. With them, I moved ahead with the vision with great vigor.

However, I again failed to notice what was happening with my core leadership. They weren't on board. Maybe my head was in the sand. Maybe I wasn't listening. Maybe they didn't have the courage to state their minds. Or perhaps it was a mixture of all of the above. But a slow, rising tension began to engulf the church. Other members of the church were even accusing the leadership of not having the courage to confront me. No one trusted anyone else. Everything was grinding to a halt. My leadership was in trouble.

To be candid, I wanted to quit. Everything was failing. I was frustrated and tired. I didn't want to continue the fight. Yet amidst this struggle, I remembered the very important leadership secret Coach Smith taught me years earlier: make failure your friend. Look at your mistake, learn from it, and move on.

So when I finally realized the problem, I knew I had two options. I could continue to steamroll ahead and let the chips fall where they might. Or I could stop, go in front of the people, apologize for my mistakes, and seek their input.

I chose the latter. I recommitted myself to leadership. I devised a plan to find unity, a vision both staff and leadership could buy and support. I met with each lay leader for at least an hour, often more. I asked his opinion of what had happened. I quizzed him regarding how I had failed. I intently listened. I took copious notes. I told each one that anything about me or the staff was fair game. I really wanted to know what they were thinking.

Then, over the next several months, we got the lay and paid leadership together. With the help of a church member skilled in conflict management, we got people talking with one another. When they did, we were surprised to find that most of the problems were blown way out of proportion. The mistrust that had formed between us began to dissolve.

After several months of healthy dialogue, I then recommitted myself to them as a servant leader. I told them I wanted a common vision, one on which we all could mutually agree and enthusiastically support. I told them that if they wanted to tear to shreds the previous vision and start all over again, I would be willing to do that. Amazingly, they all looked at me and said, "You're the leader, lead us!" So we went over the vision again, took out some areas of weakness, and added other items that made it stronger. We ended with a stronger vision statement that could now be taken to the congregation with total unity.

Was it hard? Absolutely! Who enjoys eating crow? But I did regain their trust. When I retreated, consensus started building. Soon the church moved ahead with enthusiasm. Amazing growth began to occur, largely from those who had never gone to church.

That all happened several years ago. Today this church is one of the healthiest, fastest growing in the area. It is a purpose-driven organization. People genuinely care for one another as at no other time in my leadership here. Throughout the organization, people clearly know what we're about. The vision is easily articulated by almost everyone.

We learned through a very difficult episode that failure should not be feared. When properly approached, it can be one of life's best teaching tools.

Where There's a Way, There's a Will

Jim Valvano, the late coach of North Carolina State University, loved to tell this story about Coach Smith and the 1982 national championship game against Georgetown. During the timeout, with 30-plus seconds to go and UNC down by one point, Valvano was having fun with the Carolina fans surrounding him. He offered all of them different offensive strategies to score the winning basket and then stop Georgetown on its ensuing possession. One particular fan kept responding to each of Valvano's strategies, "Dean will find a way."

As most fans know, Michael Jordan scored the go-ahead basket with 16 seconds left. As Georgetown came down the court, Freddie Brown accidentally threw the ball to James Worthy; Carolina won the game.

Valvano stared incredulously at Brown's errant pass. Then the UNC fan tugged on his sleeve as the final buzzer sounded Carolina's victory. "See," he said, "I told you Dean would find a way!"

One of the ways Coach Smith always found a way was through the avenue of failure. It didn't scare him. It didn't intimidate him. It didn't cause him to worry. He simply embraced it and learned whatever he needed to know. The failure made him better.

Failure also made his players better, even Michael Jordan. Jordan once said: "I missed more than nine thousand shots in my career. I've lost almost three hundred games. Twenty-six times I've been trusted to take the game-winning shot, and missed. I've failed over and over and over again in my life. And that is why I succeed."

Jordan, like Coach Smith had found a way to make failure his friend. It's one of Coach Smith's secrets to success, and he wanted me to make sure I told you!

Thought for the Day

***When faced with failure, recognize it,
admit it, learn from it, forget it.***

Game Plan

• Do not fear failure — everyone makes mistakes

• Learn from your mistakes and move on

• Keep trying to find a way — there is one

Team Practice

• How do you deal with your mistakes?

• How do you help others learn from their mistakes?

• How does your organization deal with mistakes?

• What can your organization do to
encourage learning from failure?

KNOW WHO REALLY IS IN CONTROL

"There have been many times in life when I've had to give up."

I used to have a favorite illustration about Winston Churchill, the esteemed prime minister of Great Britain. His skillful leadership kept England steady during the incessant battering of German air raids during World War II.

It seems that Churchill graduated in the bottom third of his school class. There was absolutely nothing special about his scholarship or leadership back then. But many years later, as prime minister, his alma mater invited him to give the commencement address. The story is that he walked to the podium and told the students, "Never give up. Never, ever, ever give up." And then he sat down. The stunned audience eventually broke into an uproarious ovation.

For decades, ministers and speakers have used this anecdote about Churchill to motivate people to keep on trying when faced with adversity. It used to be one of my favorites, too, until Coach Smith readjusted my thinking about it.

When I told him how much I liked the tale, he responded, "David, I hate that story."

"But why?" I just had to ask. I was puzzled that this master motivator would loathe an example of dogged determination that paid off in eventual victory.

"Because I have learned in my life that many times I have had to give up," he replied, "and give it to God."

As I reflected on this statement, I realized its truth. Sometimes you *do* have to give up; there's simply nothing else to do but to quit trying and realize that, ultimately, you are not in control.

Few people know just how difficult those early years were for Dean Smith as the head coach of North Carolina. He wasn't the winningest coach in college basketball back then; he lost a lot of games and became the frequent butt of jokes. Art Heyman, Duke's All-American during Smith's first two seasons, was amazed when he discovered how revered Smith had become. "Dean Smith?" he said. "Why, he was the biggest joke around."

Frank McGuire, under whom Coach Smith served as an assistant, used to joke about his name, taking a dig at a person he thought to be rather drab, a person of gray anonymity: "Dean? What's that? A guy's not named Dean. He becomes a dean!"

Larry Brown, probably the best player on those early teams, said, "I don't know many men who could have gone through those first few years." When Coach Smith was hung in effigy, the question on everyone's mind changed from "will he leave?" to "when will he leave, and who will be his replacement?"

During this painful time, Coach Smith's sister gave him a book by Catherine Marshall called *Beyond Ourselves*. He is particularly close to his sister, and she has a keen interest in spirituality and theology.

Helplessness Is an Asset

Coach Smith focused on one particular chapter, titled "The Power of Helplessness." He began to see how little in life he really could control.

Winston Churchill's very short, very dramatic never-give-up speech may be great fodder for motivational speakers, but life had taught Dean Smith that it simply wasn't true.

"Crisis brings us face to face with our inadequacy," Catherine Marshall wrote, "and our inadequacy in turn leads us to the inexhaustible sufficiency of God." That described exactly where Smith was: face to face with his inadequacy. "No sinner is hopeless; no situation is irretrievable. No cause is past redeeming," she said. "Helplessness is actually one of the greatest assets a human being can have...the crucible out of which victory could rise." Catherine Marshall's book had Coach Smith's full attention.

Before the next game against Duke in Durham, he gave a spirited talk to the team. That was unusual; it's just not his style to give fiery pep talks. But he motivated the players that day, and Carolina beat Duke, 65–62. Two years later he made his first Final Four.

No one but Coach Smith knows exactly what happened during those days after he was hung in effigy. In an article written about him in the magazine of the Fellowship of Christian Athletes, he refers to this tumultuous time in his life. He reflected how he went home after all this turmoil and told God that he had given his life to Him many years before. Now he was giving Him everything, basketball included.

He learned an important truth that many great leaders have learned in the darkest days of adversity: key men need to learn who really holds the keys.

Coach Smith recounted for me that time when he totally gave it all up and turned it over to God. It's a habit he still has. "I don't want to act like a saint, for I am not one," he told me. "But deep down, every day, I try to turn it all over to a higher power. I know I have to let go and let God guide me every day.

"I try to set some kind of example as a professing Christian, but I realize I fall far short. I choose the Christian faith because I know I am weak. I need help for strength and guidance. Of course, I believe all humans were created to feel inferior and weak until we creatures make contact with the Creator and learn that He is in control."

Life holds mysteries that only God understands. Coach Smith comprehends that. He realizes, as many of us do, that the most frequently spoken word in heaven is probably going to be "oh," when God reveals to us why He did what He did.

The philosophy that it is sometimes necessary to give up is summed up in one of Coach Smith's favorite prayers. It's called the Serenity Prayer, and he often gives a copy of it to people. Almost everyone is familiar with the first part of this prayer by Reinhold Niebuhr; here is the full version.

> God, grant me the serenity to accept
> the things I cannot change,
> Courage to change the things I can,
> And wisdom to know the difference —
>
> Living one day at a time,
> Enjoying one moment at a time,
> Accepting hardship as the pathway to peace;
>
> Taking, as He did, this sinful world
> As it is, not as I would have it;
> Trusting that He will make all things right
> If I surrender to His will;
>
> That I may be reasonably happy in this life,
> and supremely happy with Him forever in the next.
> Amen.

Coach Smith always had a "thought for the day" typed at the head of each practice schedule. One of these little nuggets reads, "If you can't do something about a problem, it's a fact of life." Sounds like the Serenity Prayer, doesn't it? Accepting the things we cannot change is an important leadership principle.

Roots of Faith

Dean Smith was raised in a relatively strict family and church environment. His parents sowed the seeds of faith in his life at an early age.

They demanded that he attend Sunday services, sometimes spending most of the day at church. He went to youth camps at Ottawa University. During his high school and college years, his family belonged to the First Baptist Church of Topeka, Kansas.

Although his beliefs are no longer expressed in the strictness of his familial background, he still tenaciously holds to his faith in God. When Smith first moved to Chapel Hill, he joined a group of 25 people who began a new church in the area. The group committed themselves to racial justice and being a part of the lives of hurting people. That was the beginning, in the spring of 1959, of the Binkley Baptist Church. That congregation has had a tremendous effect on Coach Smith and his faith.

He attends church weekly, win or lose. He readily understands what Christianity is supposed to be about; therefore, he often gently criticizes the church at large for castigating wounded people, for not loving them unconditionally. He teases me that Alcoholics Anonymous probably understands how to create a loving community better than the church does.

"The purpose of the church," he said, "is to give people strength so they can move on with their lives. In my own congregation, we very much see it as a church headquarters. We gain strength from each other. Consequently, many of our members are in politics, and many are involved in bringing about social change. That's what the church should be doing — caring for one another so we can help a hurting world."

Although I am a pastor, I do not become defensive when he criticizes the church in this way. Dean Smith is right. It's all too easy for members of a church to get caught up in taking care of their own people to the neglect of the hurting souls all around them.

Sociologist Tony Campolo, who is often critical of the church, is a challenge and an inspiration to Dean Smith. Campolo urges followers of Jesus Christ to be concerned with the needs of the poor and oppressed worldwide while developing their own personal spirituality. Coach Smith has given me many of his tapes through the years, often saying to me, "You really need to hear this one!"

Yet his faith is also very private. Smith is not ostentatious about anything in his life. He follows the example recorded in Matthew 6 of Jesus, who instructed His followers to pray and give their money away, but to do it in secret. Smith desires no earthly recognition for what he believes is the right thing to do. He once said to me, "You know, David, you and I have the toughest jobs in the state of North Carolina. People vicariously live through how we perform. If we do well, they feel good about themselves. If we don't, they don't. Isn't that sad? Only God should be able to do that to our insides."

Expressions of Faith

After Carolina defeated Georgetown in 1982 for the national championship, Coach Smith gave some interesting insights into his faith in an interview with Wendy Ryan. He complained that athletic competition produces what our society calls winners and losers. "Those terms," he said, "certainly have different connotations which, in my opinion, isn't good. The 'loser' and those associated with losing sometimes feel bad, and the 'winners' have external affirmation for the wrong reasons. I don't think our Creator meant for one person or one group, the 'losers,' to feel bad in order for another group or individual to feel superior.

"The total emphasis on winning versus participation is the problem," he continued. "Why doesn't the Christian church invite the guy who dropped four touchdown passes to come and talk about his faith? The fact that so many want to interview me after the national championship instead of when our team has a bad year is an example of what I'm addressing. The Christian culture has adopted the secular culture's ideas of success."

In one of my meetings with Coach Smith, he related the story of a boxer who observed his opponent at prayer just before a match. The boxer anxiously asked his trainer if it meant anything. "Not if he can't fight," the trainer replied.

Coach Smith often struggles with athletes who credit God with all their success. "I have to admit that it bothers me when a Christian calls on the Lord as a celestial bellhop," he said. "Of course, a pro athlete may indeed perform better because his life-style as a Christian helps overcome anxieties experienced by other players. However, constant practice would help his performance the most.

"If Christianity promised a 'magic wand' to receive everything one wishes — such as perfect health or a perfect performance — one would choose Christianity for the wrong reasons. I believe God created each human being to have freedom of choice. If I choose to smoke three packs of cigarettes a day, then I should not blame God if I have lung cancer some day. If some drunken driver crosses the middle line and kills my son or daughter, I don't think that is God's will; it's the wrong choice of the other to drink and drive. So, if some athlete intercepts a crucial pass, that athlete has made a choice to practice and to use his talent. The quarterback throwing the pass may have prayed to have it completed."

One of Coach Smith's favorite authors, Robert McAfee Brown, said this about our freedom of choice: it is like we are all in a symphony, sometimes choosing wrong notes, and God, the Conductor, can still make beautiful music.

Although he is often open about his faith, Dean Smith would never force his faith on others. He honors their freedom of choice. He respects players from the Jewish faith. Within the last several years, he has had a couple of players with Muslim backgrounds. However, he did believe in what Danish philosopher and theologian Soren Kierkegaard called "the indirect witness." In his "thoughts for the day," published at the top of every practice plan, Coach Smith always tried to plant a seed that would last for a lifetime in the players' minds, something that could be all-inclusive for all faith perspectives.

James Worthy, one of Carolina's greatest players, remembers that Coach Smith used to be very open about conversation regarding his faith and seeing how his players' faith was developing. "But it wasn't something he forced on us," Worthy noted. "We said the Lord's Prayer before every game. That was a reminder to us, because in college you tend to forget those parts of your life. You aren't consistent with the way you were brought up. He was reminding us not to forget our roots.

"And before every meal he would mention faith. Because he wanted to remind us that something could always happen and we aren't in control."

Dean Smith sees coaching as a calling from God, in the classic sense of the word *vocation*. "My pastor, Dr. Robert Seymour," he said, "has helped me understand that any vocation is acceptable to God if it involves work that is necessary in God's world or work that makes a positive contribution to man's well-being and happiness. There is no double standard between sacred vocations and secular ones. Once I thought I had reneged on my promise to God to put Him first by pursuing a career in coaching. But now I know I can faithfully serve God as a coach."

Realities of Faith

After the 1982 national championship, Frank DeFord wrote an article about Coach Smith in *Sports Illustrated*. In the article DeFord explored why a few coaches felt Coach Smith was not real. One coach had even said, "The man and the image don't match."

DeFord spent a good bit of the piece examining Coach Smith's religious convictions, which go back to his Kansas upbringing. DeFord then pointed out how he thinks these spiritual roots were incompatible with Smith's divorce in the early '70s, the fact that he was a chain smoker, and that he enjoyed a glass of Scotch. He suggested this collision of faith with real life helped create an image, at least for some, of hypocrisy.

However, DeFord failed to realize several points of faith that frame Coach Smith's life. First, he never wanted to be seen as a saint. His faith became real to him through trials, but he still realized the constant struggle we all have in wanting to become what we are not.

Second, Coach Smith has never adhered to a rigid, fundamentalist position. He honors those who have chosen this path, but it is not one with which he is comfortable. The church he attends in Chapel Hill wears a "liberal" label. His Protestant Christianity never suggests that drinking is bad. Drunkenness is, and Coach Smith stands against that. But drinking alcohol itself is not against his religious convictions.

Third, he believes that faith is a journey. He does not believe he will ever be perfect in this life. He has never tried to be anything other than what he presents himself to be.

But DeFord also failed to realize that Coach Smith desires to learn from his mistakes and do better. Yes, his first marriage ended in divorce. It was an extraordinarily painful time. Yet he remains friends with his ex-wife, and they worked out a meaningful way of being involved with their children together. Moreover, his second marriage is solid, a loving union that produced two fine daughters. His mistress is basketball, and it may have cost him his first marriage; it hasn't his second.

As for smoking, he quit. Cold turkey. He knew it was destroying his health, so he abruptly stopped.

Does he still have foibles, besetting problems with which he struggles? Of course! We all do. But my purpose in these paragraphs is to point out how important his faith really is. It is my opinion that his faith informs practically all of the principles we have been addressing.

Foundation of Faith

Without understanding Coach Smith's faith perspective, you can't really understand why and how he operates. Consider these examples.

Why is he so loyal to his players? Why does he put them first? I think it's birthed in a spiritual conviction that we are to live this life first of all for others.

Why does he demand racial equality? It's because of his conviction that all people are created equal in God's sight; therefore we must do everything possible to make sure people are appropriately and fairly treated. Why did he begin recruiting black athletes in the mid-1960s? "When I became the coach at Carolina," he said, "my pastor advised me that I should recruit a black athlete. He thought most vocations are and should be *Christian* vocations, and as the coach my first responsibility in my Christian vocation was to have a black athlete in a predominately white southern university."

Why is cheating simply not an option for him? He has a firm conviction that taking what does not belong to you is wrong, and that the necessity of telling the truth is an immutable law of the universe, created by God to be obeyed by His creatures.

Why is the team more important than the individual? It's because of his conviction that community is very important. He believes that God created us to live together, and one way that can be learned and demonstrated is through team play.

Why care for the poor and oppressed? He follows the biblical example of feeding and clothing the hungry and reaching out to those who are suffering. His conviction is that we are all citizens of the world and responsible for one another.

Why not give into failure? It's because of the conviction that God is the God of the second chance.

Why is he such a positive encourager? It's because he has felt the positive encouragement from God to keep on going, even when the odds seem overwhelming.

Why the emphasis on self-effacement and humility? Because humility is one of the earmarks of the Christian faith and it therefore needs to be practiced as a way of life.

The list could go on and on. If you fail to understand Coach Smith's faith, you cannot understand the principles by which he lives. He believes God created the universe with certain underlying principles that define reality. God set them in motion and obeys them Himself. Coach Smith simply discovered them and used them in his own leadership.

Overriding Life Principle

One year Coach Smith and his wife spent each Thursday during the Lenten season with other church members studying a book entitled *Unconditional Love* by Father J.S. Powell. Powell asked a question in that book that had profound implications for his life: what is your overriding life principle?

"For some people," Smith said to me, "it is money, to some it is power, to others it isn't clearly defined as they look inward. The question I have studied is, 'What should be the motivation for turning a life over to God, or essentially to be a Christian?'... I have believed that the motivation for the Christian faith is gratitude. Gratitude for love and acceptance by God. Gratitude for forgiveness. Gratitude for giving us life.

"We can pray for and acknowledge gratefully the many resources of strength and courage and alertness which we receive as the gifts of God....Thus, as Christian laymen with athletic interests and talents, we see that anything we do, we do because God qualifies us to do it as we respond to the gifts he has given. Each of us then has a sacred calling."

A friend of mine in Charlotte is Greg Keith, a very successful developer who was a high school All-American and recruited by many schools across America, North Carolina included. Keith recently shared with me a conversation he had with Coach Smith during the recruiting process. Coach Smith said to him, "You know, Greg, you can't take God out to dinner, or to a sporting event, or any other place. But there is one thing you can always do for God and that's love His children. Whenever you do something good for His children, you are serving Him."

Keith remembers something else Coach Smith said: "God is sovereign over His universe. I am not in charge. He is. It rains on the just and the unjust. We're all returning to dust one day. Until then, we simply do the best we can for other people."

This is the kind of faith that allowed Dean Smith to withstand the critics for 36 years.

It's the foundation for caring for others before himself, placing the team before the individual, and building personal character. It's essential to understanding his greatness and effectiveness as a leader.

It's rooted in the wisdom of knowing when to give in and give it to God.

Thought for the Day

Helplessness can actually be an asset,
the crucible out of which victory can rise.

Game Plan

- Accept the fact that you can't control everything

- Have a sense of God

- Discover your vocation, your sacred calling

- Let your faith permeate your life

- Never force your faith on others

Team Practice

- What does having a sense of God mean to you?

- How do you demonstrate your spiritual beliefs in your personal life?

- How do your spiritual values impact your behavior at work?

- What role does spirituality play in your organization's success?

THE MARATHON
OF INFLUENCE

"It's daily living that really matters."

The Tar Heels had just suffered a heartbreaking loss in the first round of the NCAA tournament in 1979. On the bus ride back to Chapel Hill, a great silence fell over the passengers. The sense of failure for the highly ranked Tar Heels consumed the players' attention.

What did Coach Smith do? He went to the back and spoke to Ged Doughton, who had just played his last collegiate game.

"Come by the office first thing Monday morning, Ged, and let's start talking about your future."

That's typical of Dean Smith. Putting failure behind him, putting his players and their future first. Coaching for the long haul, not just a winning season.

Contrast his style of long-term leadership with someone like Al "Chain Saw" Dunlap. A month shy of his second anniversary as embattled Sunbeam's supposed savior, Dunlap was fired as chairman and CEO during a weekend meeting. The chairman who followed Dunlap said, "We lost confidence in his leadership."

Dunlap entered Sunbeam as a corporate superstar with a reputation for turning around a corporation with a sagging performance. How did he receive the nickname "Chain Saw"? He was known for coming into a corporation and slashing thousands of workers in a cost-cutting effort during his 15-year career. He prefers to be called "Rambo in pinstripes," but the expression "dunlaping" became a synonym for downsizing and layoffs.

At Scott Paper, where he cut a third of the workforce, the company's stock tripled during his 18-month tenure. Sunbeam's shares soared nearly 60 percent the day Dunlap's hiring was announced. At Sunbeam, Dunlap cut 6000 jobs, half the workforce. He shut down 18 of 26 factories.

When word of Dunlap's firing spread, none of Sunbeam's former workers felt sad. In fact, they couldn't hide their happiness. They were ecstatic that the "Chain Saw" had been sawed in two.

Some of the 500 workers laid off from an iron and toaster plant Dunlap closed in Louisiana were "doing cartwheels," said Gary Elliot, a former maintenance manager. He said, "You never want to gloat when someone is terminated, but he affected a lot of lives here. Ours was a profitable plant. He closed it purely to boost the stock. He got what he deserved."

Dunlap is not the only corporate superstar whose brilliance has faded. A physicist who had previously turned around ailing National Semiconductor, Gilbert Amelio lasted 17 months at Apple before being fired and tagged with the label "plodder and technocrat."

AT&T President John Walter, after much previous success, lasted only nine months, unable to build consensus and gain the support of the board.

Hollywood's super-agent, Michael Ovitz, was sacked by Disney after a short time. In the midst of Wall Street's bull market, you must have a corporate scapegoat when performance is lackluster. No CEO seems safe.

It's interesting that, shortly after joining Sunbeam, Dunlap told an interviewer that if a company couldn't be fixed in a year, it couldn't be fixed. He displayed the same arrogance in the title of his book about corporate restructuring: *Mean Business: How I Save Bad Companies and Make Good Companies Great.*

After Dunlap's dismissal, Sunbeam told its workers and shareholders that management was determined to turn things around. But one official, in trying to encourage people, asked for patience. He said, "We're in absolutely no hurry. We are long-term players."

A Contrast in Leadership

Long-term players versus corporate quick-fixers. That's the contrast in leadership between a "corporate genius" like Al Dunlap and long-term leader like Dean Smith. Dunlap was concerned about the profit line first, people second. Coach Smith was concerned about people first and wins second. Dunlap loved the spotlight and claimed it whenever possible. Coach Smith shied away from public adulation, always wanting the players and the team to receive it.

Dunlap looked for immediate results — fix it in one year, he said, or it can't be fixed. Coach Smith was a leader for the long haul, patiently, year after year, building his foundation on the core values of people first, the team above the individual, and personal character. Dunlap was nicknamed "Chain Saw" by his work associates and peers. Coach Smith was and is affectionately called "Coach."

What was the result of these two different styles of leadership? Dunlap was fired in disgrace; his underlings despised him. Coach Smith coached for 36 years and retired with universal acclaim; his underlings adored him.

Coach Smith understood that great leadership is a slow, steady process. And he stayed put in one place for long-haul leadership. Both Pat Riley, who coaches the Miami Heat, and Rick Pitino, head coach of the Boston Celtics, have recently written books on leadership. I've read both, and they are very good. However, the major difference between their styles of leadership and Coach Smith's is that Riley and Pitino have moved three or four times in the last 15 years. That's not necessarily wrong. But when you're in one place for 36 years and consistently practice positive leadership principles, you affect people for a lifetime.

W. Edwards Deming, whose principles transformed Japan from the post-World War II rubble to a contemporary economic superpower, says that we must first have a purpose or a mission and that it must have constancy.

Sam Walton, the founder of Wal-Mart, said, "I have concentrated all along on building the finest retailing company that we possibly could. Creating a huge personal fortune was never particularly a goal of mine."

That was Coach Smith. Successful leaders are building values and principles lived out over a long time. Walton says his success really began about 20 years into the business. He didn't look for windows of opportunity, but steadfast obedience over the long haul to his core values.

Since I have been the pastor of one church for 19 years, I've baptized babies, confirmed them, married them, and then baptized their own babies. It develops into a beautiful long-term relationship with a congregation, and an ability to impact people that only comes with being there for the long haul. People have the opportunity not only to hear your words but to see you live them.

Which has the greatest impact — long-haul leaders or quick-fixers? Obviously, leadership over the long-term impacts the most people and impacts them to a greater degree. As Collins and Porras point out in *Built to Last*, nearly all of the early leaders of visionary companies stayed at the helm for long periods of time (an average of 32.4 years). I believe Coach Smith led for the present team he was coaching, but also for the next generation, and the next!

A part of Coach Smith's genius is that his leadership was not a sprint, but a marathon. He was consistent, and he led with long-term goals in mind. And when he retired, it was on his own terms. He left on top. People did not want him to retire. They wanted him to coach for as long as he wanted.

Moreover, and this has been too often overlooked, he left the cupboard full for his dear friend and long-time associate, Bill Guthridge. Look closely at the way Coach Smith's retirement unfolded. All his leadership secrets shine forth again. Reciprocal loyalty. Putting people first. The team above the individual. Personal integrity and character.

Notice also he endorsed someone who shares his core values and will continue to live them throughout his contract. That's why I'm convinced Coach Guthridge's successor will also be someone in Coach Smith's domain. This insures the values that built the organization for his 36 years will continue to lead Carolina basketball for decades to come.

Many today marvel at Jack Welch's leadership at General Electric. But he was raised in GE. He knew the culture, vision and values. His successor will probably be a similar choice. In 1991, Welch said, "From now on, [choosing my successor] is the most important decision I'll make. It occupies a considerable amount of thought almost every day."

That's how Wal-Mart, 3M, Boeing, IBM, Johnson and Johnson, Mereck, and many other visionary companies have staying power and influence over the long haul. It's why Carolina basketball will continue to be successful well into the twenty-first century.

Leaving at the Right Time

Coach Smith's retirement did not catch his former boss, athletic director John Swofford, by surprise. For the last several years Smith had evaluated whether he had the energy and enthusiasm necessary for his players to do their best under his leadership. He had always said he would retire when October rolled around and he didn't feel he could give the team and the individual players what they needed to succeed. Finally, in October of 1997, he didn't sense that excitement and announced his retirement. Swofford said, "He did it just like he said he would. His entire life has been first class. He had to go out on top."

What does it mean for a leader to retire at the right time? Swofford said, "Whenever we talked about his retirement, he would say every time that it was really important to him that he leave the program in good shape."

Leaving the program in good shape meant several things. First of all, from Coach Smith's perspective, it meant leaving the program in better shape than when he began as a leader. Looking back to 1961, when he became the head coach, that certainly occurred. The program is in much better shape now. Every effective leader should be able to see that kind of marked improvement.

Second, it meant leaving the cupboard full for his successor. Coach Smith has a deep and abiding friendship with Bill Guthridge. He wanted Coach Guthridge to have the job after his retirement both to reward him for all the years of faithful support and to give him a chance to earn enough money in a short period of time to insure his financial security. However, and perhaps even more important to Coach Smith, was to allow his loyal associate to succeed at the same level or perhaps even a greater level of success than he had.

John Kilgo, editor of *Carolina Blue* athletics magazine, is absolutely convinced that Coach Smith would not have retired in October 1997 if Antawn Jamison had decided to go professional after his sophomore year. When Jamison returned for his junior year, Coach Smith knew the team would be very good. The year before they had gone to the Final Four and four of the five starters were returning. Yet without Antawn, the team certainly would not have been as good. Kilgo believes that Coach Smith would have persevered through another season until the team would have been excellent enough to pass on to Coach Guthridge.

After Coach Smith's retirement was announced, Henry Araton wrote in *The New York Times*: "Of course Dean Smith has never admitted this, never will, but the coach with a record of 879 wins turned what might have been a grand farewell tour with a championship cherry on top into an extraordinary show of appreciation for a man who stayed by his side for thirty years. Smith thanked Bill Guthridge for his assistance in a way so many others in this look-at-me industry absolutely could not. Telling a half-truth that he was too tired to continue, Smith gave Guthridge a team to run with....To many, Smith was the 1997 Sportsman-of-the Year after breaking Adolph Rupp's record of 877 victories before losing to Arizona in the national semifinals. One year later, without being part of a single game, Dean Smith looks like a bigger sportsman than ever."

This says much about Dean Smith's character, doesn't it? In a day when coaches jump to the next university in order to receive the largest amount of money and acclaim possible in the shortest amount of time, here is an example of longevity, perseverance, success, and a concern that his successor experience equal benefits. Even in his retirement, Coach Smith was putting others first.

That was one of his major core values. It drove him. Like Walt Disney, who left his core values in place, allowed Michael Eisner and the new Disney team to resurge with prosperous success in the 1990s.

Contrast Disney to Columbia Pictures and its head, Harry Cohn. After his death in 1958, Cohn did not have these core ideologies in place. He didn't care first for people, and his funeral represented a Dunlap-like relief that he was gone. Someone at the funeral supposedly said that 1300 people came not to mourn his death but to make sure he was dead! Columbia limped along and finally ceased to exist as an independent company, rescued in 1973, eventually sold to Coca-Cola.

On April 11, 1997, headlines in the Chapel Hill daily newspaper proclaimed a startling announcement: Molly Corbett Broad became the first woman ever appointed to head the University of North Carolina's 16-campus system in the school's 200-plus-year tradition.

When asked about her leadership style, she said she followed the example set many years before by her faculty advisor, who was later a university chancellor and eventually one of her closest friends. "He was a great mentor," she said, "and in today's vernacular he would be called a 'servant leader.'" Broad continued to explain, "His style was very humble, but he had a very strong conviction that his assignment was to turn the university over to his successor better, stronger, and healthier than he had received it."

I would imagine that Molly Broad sincerely appreciated Dean Smith's retirement. I only wish she could have watched his leadership. I believe it would have profoundly impacted her, as her chancellor friend similarly did.

When it comes to knowing when is the right time to leave, here are some questions that naturally arise.

Is the organization I am presently heading better now than when I first became its leader? If not, why not?

If it is better, what's the next stage to which my leadership is being called? Is it in this organization? Is it to another work?

Am I nearing the time to retire? Am I still feeling the same passion for my work?

Am I giving my work associates and my team my best energy? If that energy is beginning to wane, when should I step down?

Who should my successor be? Am I choosing a time for retirement that gives him or her the best opportunity to succeed, perhaps even beyond my own success?

After Coach Smith's retirement, Bill Guthridge gave me these insights regarding why Coach Smith finally retired. "He just didn't have the energy to coach the 1997–98 team that he knew it needed. And I think a lot of those energies went to former players and in many respects that just wore him down. I personally don't know how he lasted as long as he did. Because of the number of people that he cared about and was trying to help out overwhelmed him.

"When I was his assistant, I deferred as much of that as I could so he could concentrate on the big things, but I couldn't shield him from everything. No one knows the demands on his time, the long hours of work and the people he genuinely cares for. I don't know of another person who could have managed all of this, but he did."

Perhaps one of Coach Smith's most meaningful letters he received upon announcement of his retirement came from Dickson Gribble, a former player from his first seasons as head coach at North Carolina and presently a colonel in the United States Army. He wrote:

> Coach Smith,
>
> I am saddened by your retirement, but understand. As my own mandatory retirement date (30 years active duty) soon approaches, I often reflect on what's next. You alone know when you are ready — you alone. I admire you for knowing when it was time and doing it the way you did.
>
> Having been a part of an organization and a culture for so long that passes leadership, I reflect on it often. And I am often asked to speak about it. Even in military work, I use you often as my example. Note I didn't say always, in that I have had my life also cross with Colin Powell's. I cite your commitment to excellence, to integrity, and to caring for others as specific traits worthy of emulation. I often note your commitment to equal opportunity has been a part of the Carolina program since during the days of Willie Cooper and Charlie Scott.

I also talk about the importance of teamwork in my successful organization — be it on the sports field or battlefield. People understanding their role — as a soldier, civilian, point guard, or bench player. At Carolina, you taught us that we all had a role and to fill that role to the best of our ability for the overall benefit of the team. Thanks for that.

On his deathbed, Walt Disney purportedly was giving counsel to another leader about how to make Florida's Disney World more successful. I can imagine Coach Smith doing something like that, on his deathbed, giving the present head coach insights into how to make UNC's basketball program even more successful. That's because he sees leadership for the long haul, not just for one year or several seasons.

As news of Coach Smith's retirement spread around the university, hundreds of students gathered outside the Smith Center. At the press conference to officially announce the retirement, they all chanted, "Four more years! Four more years!"

It was a fitting tribute to a coach who knew, perhaps better than anyone else, that winning wasn't nearly as important as how you play the game.

Thought for the Day

Leadership is a marathon, not a sprint.

Game Plan

• Think of influencing people over a lifetime

• Plan for your successor

• Know when to leave

• Leave your successor with success

• Imagine what people will feel at
your retirement...and funeral

Team Practice

• What actions do you take to
change daily inconsistencies?

• What should be done to plan for a successor?

• When should that be?

• Would your successor succeed?

• How would your underlings feel at
your retirement and/or funeral?

AFTERWORD

When talking to different people for this project, I concluded each interview with this question: "Pretend Coach Smith is right here in front of you. You now have the opportunity to tell him anything you desire. What would you say to him?"

Here are their answers.

"Coach Smith, I've always told you I've appreciated you. I also want to say I love you for what you have done in my life. It's meant a lot to me and to generations of young people who will be influenced by the people you have touched."

—**Bobby Jones**
athletic director and head basketball coach
Charlotte Christian High School
Charlotte, North Carolina

"Thank you for the impact you have had on my life, from the first day I walked into your office to this moment. I want to say 'Thank you' because everything that I do in terms of my professional career I look back and think what would you do, then I try to do it like you."

—**Justin Kurault**
former team manager

"You are like a father figure to me, someone I really care about. I can't adequately express how much I appreciate you. God has used you in my life. I give God the glory, but He used you to get my marriage back in order and for me to be the right father to my children. You have even helped me out of some difficult financial situations. The best way I can say 'thank you' is to keep my life disciplined and to leave situations better than when I first got there."

—Al Wood
former UNC All-American

"Dean, you're an inspiration to so many of us and I appreciate what you represent not only to intercollegiate athletics, but what you represent as a human being."

—John Swofford
commissioner
Atlantic Coast Conference

"I have always been surprised about the absolute reverence your former players have when they speak about you. When I spend time with you, I want to spend more time with you. When I am around you, I feel your goodness, your honesty. Thank you for who you are."

—Jerry West
general manager
Los Angeles Lakers

"You are an amazing person. I know you don't want to take the credit, but there are a few of us out here that you are responsible for making us who we are. I love you like a father and I love you like a brother. And I just want to say thank you. You are the man!"

—James Worthy
former UNC All-American

"I am hoping to be a head coach one day, and I hope I can be one-hundredth of the man you are. I hope I can instill in my players all the values and all those characteristics that you instilled in me. I hope I can teach them about loyalty, friendship, integrity, and how to win and lose graciously, about saying nice things about other people, about saying thank you. Thank you for all you have done for me."

> **—Pat Sullivan**
> former UNC player

"Thank you for a terrific ride that you've let me go on with a lot of your teams and a lot of your different players. But more than that, thank you for what you've taught me about life in general. And how to be fair with people. You've taught me how to say things to people they may not want to hear but need to hear. Thank you for your compliments of my broadcasting. Thanks so very much for all you've done for me and all the young people who have played for you and all you've done for the university. It certainly would not be what it is today without your input."

> **—Woody Durham**
> "Voice of the Tar Heels"

"On behalf of all the coaches, players, trainers, secretaries, doctors, and anybody that has ever had a chance to associate with you, thank you. I don't know how you found the time to do it. To be such a good person in this profession is very difficult to do. It just shows what a wonderful human being you are."

> **—Eddie Fogler**
> head coach
> University of South Carolina

"Well, first, I want to thank you very much for giving me an opportunity just to be a part of the North Carolina family. I also want to thank you for contributing so much to so many people's lives. You probably can't imagine how many lives you have touched, how special you are. We miss you and want you to continue to enjoy yourself because you've given so many people joy for a number of years."

> **—Jimmy Black**
> UNC starting point guard
> 1982 National Championship team

"I am a better person simply for being a part of your life. You made us all feel special. Thank you for who you are."

> **—Dave Hanners**
> assistant coach
> University of North Carolina

"Coach, you have been one of the most important people in all my life. Thank you for all you have meant to me through the years."

> **—Richard Vinroot**
> former UNC player
> former mayor of Charlotte, North Carolina

"You are a fantastic person. I would never be the person I am today if it were not for you. Thank you for all you have meant to me."

> **—Pearce Landry**
> former UNC player

"You are my friend. Your life has profoundly affected mine. Thank you for always being there for me.

> **—John Lotz**
> former assistant coach
> University of North Carolina

"I appreciate everything you have done for me. Thank you for the care and concern you have shown for my family. Thanks for the steps you have helped me take, from East Tennessee State to N.C. State to here."

> **—Buzz Peterson**
> head coach
> Appalachian State University

"No one can ever repay you for all you've meant to me and so many other people. You're an unbelievable man."

> **—John Kilgo**
> Editor
> *Carolina Blue*

"Coach, thank you for all the great experiences I had as a player and a student at the University of North Carolina. You've been great to me, and I hope you're enjoying time off with your family."

> **—Matt Doherty**
> UNC starting forward
> 1982 National Championship team
> head coach, University of Notre Dame

"Coach Smith, you have given me a lot over the years. You have helped me with major decisions in my life, and I would just like to thank you for that."

> **—Charles Waddell**
> last three-sport letterman at UNC

"I think the very best thing you can say about another person is that the more you get to know him, the more you like him. Dean, that's how I feel about you. And that's what I say to anyone who asks me about you. We're good friends and I genuinely like you, especially the more I've become acquainted with you."

—Bob Knight
head coach
Indiana University

"Coach, you're like a father to me. There is probably not a day goes by that I don't look back on my time at Carolina or a word from you that continues to help me in my life or in my family or in my community. I've always joked with my wife that the best decision I ever made was going to Carolina and she says, 'No, the best decision you ever made was marrying me.' So we get in a fight all the time because of you!"

—George Karl
head coach
Milwaukee Bucks

"I just want to say 'thank you' and that there is no way Roy Williams will ever be able to put into words what you mean to me."

—Roy Williams
head coach
Kansas University

"Coach, it's hard to pinpoint one thing. But I really don't know where I'd be today without you in my life. You're a steady rock who is always there for us. You give and give and give all the time. You do it because it is the right thing to do. You're a great basketball coach, but an even better human being."

—Phil Ford
assistant coach
University of North Carolina

"Thank you, and that's about all I know to say to you. I don't think you would want me to say much more than that. But that's enough."

> **—Bill Guthridge**
> head coach
> University of North Carolina

And, finally, I have thanks of my own to offer.

"Coach, I'm who I am today partly because of you. I'm grateful I attended North Carolina and had you as my coach. The leadership principles I use that have allowed me to grow personally and lead Forest Hill Church to a position of prosperity I learned mostly from you — directly and by observation. Thanks for caring for my mom and dad and my own family. My life has been deeply enriched by knowing you...and writing this book! Thanks again for letting me do it."

Wouldn't any leader be deeply touched by having this said by former work associates at his retirement? Why would we say this?

The answer is undoubtedly found in this final word from Dean Smith.

In my last interview with him, I invited Coach Smith to look in the camera and tell all of us any one thing he'd like to say. He paused, a wry smile crossing his face. He pointed to the camera and said, "I'd say, 'Thanks for the pass.'"

And I'd say that appropriately sums up everything in this book, wouldn't you?

INDEX